Practical Vocabulary Builder
Blackline Masters

Русский-English-Español-Français-Deutsch-Italiano-

DOROTHY GABEL LIEBOWITZ

For Teaching
Basic Second-Language Skills
In Various Languages

Illustrated by Judee Levan

National Textbook Company
a division of NTC/CONTEMPORARY PUBLISHING GROUP
Lincolnwood, Illinois USA

To the teacher:
    The blackline masters in this book are
designed to be photocopied for classroom
use only.

ISBN: 0-8442-9018-1

Published by National Textbook Company,
a division of NTC/Contemporary Publishing Group, Inc.,

10 11 12 13 VRS/VRS 0 4 3 2

PREFACE

Practical Vocabulary Builder is a companion book to *Basic Vocabulary Builder* and may be used independently or as a follow-up to the earlier book. While building and expanding upon the vocabulary of the activity areas presented in *Basic Vocabulary Builder,* the *Practical Vocabulary Builder* introduces quite a few new activity areas as well. All the word lists and the activities centered around them have as their aim to enable second language students to function effectively in everyday, "survival" contexts.

For too many years, language teachers have had to prepare their own materials to use for teaching vocabulary. Ironically, as the need for these materials increased, the time available for preparing them decreased. *Practical Vocabulary Builder* resolves this dilemma in that it is a professionally produced, inexpensive, and effective timesaver.

Practical Vocabulary Builder is a unique vehicle for teaching and reinforcing basic vocabulary whether the target language is English, Spanish, French, Italian, German, Russian, or Vietnamese. The blackline masters can be used by varying levels of students, from junior high to adult education, and by students with varying needs, from second language students to bilinguals. Not only does this book provide the teacher with handy worksheets, but it also contains many suggestions for practice and reinforcement as well as games and activities that make learning fun and effective.

The blackline masters in this book serve as inexpensive learning tools that can be used again and again in a variety of ways. These pages of simple illustrations are the building blocks for all kinds of activities that can be tailored to the interests and maturity level of the student. The vocabulary sheets can be used for coloring or writing or for more sophisticated activities like vocabulary bingo. When cut out and mounted on heavy paper or cardboard, the illustrations become mini-flashcards for easy review or testing. With a little imagination, the possibilities for using *Practical Vocabulary Builder* are endless.

The teacher's guide for each of the 32 blackline masters provides lists of the sixteen vocabulary items in the seven languages, a vocabulary supplement, teaching suggestions, and activities. The material covered in the teacher's guide may serve as a guide or springboard to further activities. Depending on the age and previous language background of the class, the teacher may want to alter the suggestions and activities to fit the students' level.

Each unit contains vocabulary that fits into a particular word group or family. For instance, one unit treats vocabulary related to the bank; another, shopping; and another, leisure activities. Although the units are numbered, they may be used in any order.

The vocabulary supplement for each unit suggests some related vocabulary the teacher may want to include or review. This supplementary vocabulary may be used in some of the activities.

The teaching suggestions section in each unit gives the teacher three exercises. The first suggests a visual preparation of the unit's sixteen vocabulary words. This is accomplished using a simple sentence with the teacher serving as the model and the students repeating the sentence. After starting with a class response, the teacher can then proceed to a small group repetition and end up with individual responses to check pronunciation and intonation. Once the class recognizes the vocabulary in the unit, you may want to do the additional substitution exercises that are suggested. These involve an alteration in the sentence structure, which may be a change of subject, verb tense, number, or a change in a pronoun or an adjective.

The second exercise presented in each teaching suggestions section is a group of questions. The teacher can use these questions to determine if the students recognize the unit's vocabulary or as an exercise to vary the original sentence presentation.

The third exercise in this section of the teacher's guide is a completion exercise. Each of the sixteen vocabulary items is given in a sentence that shows its use or meaning. The completion statements are presented in the order in which the illustrations appear on the blackline master, from left to right, top to bottom. You may want to present them in a different order to ensure that the class recognizes the vocabulary. These completion statements also serve as the foundation for some of the activities in the next section.

You also may want to use this completion exercise as the basis for a dictionary project. Have the students make a notebook with a separate page for each letter of the respective language's alphabet. As new units are covered, the class can enter the vocabulary words on the appropriate page along with a definition, a sentence, the plural form, the definite article, the indefinite article, the infinitive form, or anything you choose.

The activities section presents varying levels and types of suggested activities for using and expanding the unit's vocabulary. For the younger student there are games, such as bingo, "What am I?" and circling groups of related items. There are simple, personalized questions presented to relate the vocabulary to the individual student. For older students or those with some background knowledge of the target language, there are discussion questions, role-plays, research questions, and cultural activities. The activities may be chosen in any order, and any may be omitted depending on the students' needs and interests. The majority of the suggested activities can be done orally, but you may want to use one or more for a writing or composition exercise.

Contents

1. School

Vocabulary

English	Spanish	French	Italian	German	Russian	Vietnamese
locker	armario	casier	armadietto a chiave	Spind	стенной шкаф	tủ khóa
drinking fountain	fuente	fontaine	fontanella	Trinkbrunnen	фонтанчик	máy nước uống
science laboratory	aula de ciencias	laboratoire scientifique	laboratorio scientifico	Labor	научная лаборатория	phòng thí nghiệm hóa học
art room	aula de arte	salle des beaux arts	aula dell'arte	Kunstzimmer	кабинет искусства	phòng nghệ thuật
home economics room	aula de economía de hogar	salle des arts ménagers	aula d'economia domestica	Handwirtschaft-zimmer	кабинет домашней экономии	phòng dạy gia chánh
language laboratory	laboratorio de idiomas	laboratoire de langues	laboratorio di lingue	Sprachlabor	кабинет языка	phòng tập nghe và nói
business education room	aula de administración de empresas	salle des études commerciales	aula per studi commerciali	Zimmer für kaufmännische Ausbildung	кабинет практики	phòng học thương mại
industrial arts room, shop	aula de artes y oficios	salle des arts et métiers	aula dell'arte industriale, officina	Werkraum	кабинет труда	phòng, xưởng học kỹ nghệ
library	biblioteca	bibliothèque	biblioteca	Bibliothek	библиотека	thư viện
auditorium	auditorio	salle de conférences	auditorio	Aula	аудитория	thính đường
cafeteria	cafetería	cafétéria	tavola calda	Essraum	столовая	phòng ăn
gymnasium	gimnasio	salle de gymnastique	palestra	Turnhalle	физкультурный зал	phòng thể dục
study hall	aula de estudios	salle d'études	aula di studio	Arbeitszimmer	зал для занятий	phòng học lớn
washroom	cuarto de baño	toilettes	gabinetto	Toilette	туалет	phòng vệ sinh
office	oficina	bureau	ufficio	Büro	канцелярия	văn phòng
public address system	altavoces	haut-parleurs	altoparlante	Lautsprecheranlage	громкоговоритель, рảдиовещание	hệ thống phòng thanh

Vocabulary Supplement   subjects, courses

Teaching Suggestions

1. Point to the item and model the sentence for the students. Have them use the sentence to identify the items.

   I see a locker. (drinking fountain, science laboratory, etc.)

   I am in an art room. (home economics room, language laboratory, etc.)

   Change the subject.

   You (He, She, We, They) see (sees) a locker.

   You (He, She, etc.) are (is) in an art room.

   Change the tense.

   I was in an art room.   I saw a locker.

2. Point to a picture and ask the following questions. Direct the students to answer in a complete sentence.

   What do you see here?   What do they see here?   What did you see here?   Is she in an art room?   Are you in an art room?   Were you in an art room?

3. Complete the following with a logical answer.

   I put my jacket in a _____. (locker)
   I drink water from a _____. (drinking fountain)

   I do chemistry experiments in a _____. (science laboratory)
   I paint a picture in an _____. (art room)
   I cook dinner in the _____. (home economics room)
   I listen to Italian tapes in the _____. (language laboratory)
   I learn how to type in the _____. (business education room)
   I learn how to use tools and machines in the _____. (industrial arts room)
   I find books in the _____. (library)
   I see a play in the _____. (auditorium)
   I eat my lunch in the _____. (cafeteria)
   I play volleyball in the _____. (gymnasium)
   I do my homework in the _____. (study hall)
   I wash up and fix my hair in the _____. (washroom)
   I meet with the principal in the _____. (office)
   I listen to school announcements over the _____. (public address system)

Activities

1. Change the completion exercise in Teaching Suggestions number 3 to question form. Direct the students to write the answer on the line provided. (Where do you do chemistry experiments?)

2. What do you do with a locker? (drinking fountain, etc.) What do you do in an art room? (library, etc.)

3. What is your favorite place in school? Why?

4. What courses are taught in the science department? Foreign language, home economics, industrial arts departments, etc.?

5. Describe the art room. (science lab, etc.)

6. Play Bingo. Read the completion sentences from Teaching Suggestions number 3 as clues; the students cover the answers with pieces of paper or direct them to draw an X through them. Numerous players will win at the same time. To determine one winner, you can ask them to give the plural, a synonym, an antonym, to use the word in a complete sentence, or spell it.

7. Choose one of the classrooms. You are the teacher on the first day of class. Describe what you will be teaching.

8. Play "What am I?" This game can be played spontaneously or be prepared in advance.
   I am a room in a school.
   I have tables and chairs.
   I am filled with shelves of books.
   What am I? (library)

9. You have received an F on your report card. Explain why to your parents and tell what you will do about it.

10. Do you think boys/men should study home economics? Or girls/women a shop course?

11. What is your daily school schedule?

12. Is the educational system the same in France? Germany? How are foreign languages taught in Russia? Spain? How are the sciences taught?

13. Have you ever used your school library? Could you find a book you needed? Do libraries use the same system in other countries?

14. Prepare an announcement for your P.A. system.

15. If you took many foreign language (art, etc.) courses in school, what type of job would you be prepared for?

2. The Bank

Vocabulary

English	Spanish	French	Italian	German	Russian	Vietnamese
bank	banco	banque	banca	Bank	банк	nhà băng
teller	cajero	caissier	cassiere	Kassierer	бáнковский слýжащий	người thâu, phát tiền
officer	funcionario	cadre supérieur	funzionario	Beamter	слýжащий	cảnh-binh
guard	guarda	garde	guardia	Wächter	охрáна	người canh gác
counter	mostrador	guichet	banco	Schalter	прилáвок	bàn tính
safe-deposit box	caja de seguridad	coffre-fort	cassetta di sicurezza	Schliessfach	сейф	hộp gửi đồ quý
vault	caja fuerte	chambre forte	camera di sicurezza	Tresor	храни́лище	phòng, tủ sắt nhà băng
cash	efectivo	espèces	denaro	Bargeld	наличные дéньги	Tiền mặt
coins	monedas	monnaie	monete	Münzen, Kleingeld	монéты	đồng
coin rolls	rollos de monedas	rouleau de monnaie	rotolo di monete	Münzenrollen	свёрток монéт	Đồng tiền
check	cheque	chèque	assegno	Scheck	бáнковый чек	chi phiếu
checkbook	talonario de cheques	carnet de chèques	libretto di assegni	Scheckbuch	чéковая кни́жка	tập chi phiếu
bankbook	libreta de ahorros	carnet de banque	libretto di banca	Sparbuch	бáнковая кни́жка	sổ ghi trương mục
deposit	depósito	dépôt (d'argent)	deposito	Anzahlung	вклад	bỏ tiền vaò băng
withdrawal	retirada	retrait (d'argent)	prelevamento di fondi	Abhebung	снятие вклáда	rút tiền ra
credit card	tarjeta de crédito	carte de crédit	carta di credito	Kreditkarte	креди́тная кáрточка	thẻ tin dụng

Vocabulary Supplement   numbers, banking transactions

Teaching Suggestions

1. Point to the item and model the sentence for the students. Have them use the sentence to identify the items.
   I have a safe-deposit box. (check, etc.)
   I see a bank. (teller, guard, etc.)
   Change the above to include the number two.
   I have two safe-deposit boxes. (checks, credit cards, etc.)
   I see two banks. (tellers, guards, etc.)
2. Point to a picture and ask the following questions. Direct the students to answer in complete sentences.
   What do you have?   What does she have?   What do you see here?   Who is that?   What do they see there?   Did you have two credit cards?
3. Complete the following with a logical answer.
   A _____ is a business in which people deposit and withdraw their money. (bank)
   A _____ is a bank employee who assists customers. (teller)
   An _____ is a higher bank employee who sits at a separate desk. (officer)
   A _____ watches the bank and the money. (guard)

Before going up to the teller, customers often prepare their transactions on the _____. (counter)
Some people place their valuables in a _____. (safe-deposit box)
Money is stored in a _____. (vault)
Money as bills or coins is called _____. (cash)
Cash is in bills or _____. (coins)
Tellers usually exchange large amounts of coins in the form of _____. (coin rolls)
If you do not pay cash you may write a _____. (check)
A _____ contains blank checks and a transaction register. (checkbook)
A _____ is a record of a customer's deposits and withdrawals. (bankbook)
Putting money into an account is a _____. (deposit)
Taking money out of it is a _____. (withdrawal)
_____ are small plastic cards issued by some banks and companies which can be used to make purchases. (credit cards)

Activities

1. Change the completion statements from Teaching Suggestions number 3 to question form. (What is a bank?)
2. Change the completion statements from Teaching Suggestions number 3 to true and false statements.
3. Play Bingo. Read the completion statements from Teaching Suggestions number 3 as clues; the players cover up the answer or draw an X through the word. To determine one winner, ask the players to spell the word or to give a definition.
4. Direct the students to write the plural form of the words on the line provided.
5. Have a spelling bee using the sixteen words. As elimination rounds are required, ask the students for the plural, the definite article, the indefinite article, a demonstrative, etc.
6. Discuss the different ways to pay for an item. (cash, check, credit card)
7. Bring in a deposit and a withdrawal slip from a bank and explain how to fill them out. A neighborhood bank may be willing to supply slips.
8. Draw a blank check on the chalkboard or bring in a sample. Explain how to fill it out.
9. Set up a bank in the classroom. One student can be the guard who will answer questions and give directions; others can be a teller, customers wishing to make a deposit or withdrawal.
10. Does a bank in Russia (Italy, France, etc.) serve the same purpose as one in the United States? Does it provide any other service or function? Who owns or controls the banks?
11. If you had a safe deposit box, what would you put into it?
12. Do you have a bank account? At which bank? What type of account is it? Checking or savings?

3. Doctor and Hospital

Vocabulary

English	Spanish	French	Italian	German	Russian	Vietnamese
doctor	médico	médecin	dottore	Arzt	врач	bác sĩ
nurse	enfermera	infirmier, infirmière	infermiera	Krankenschwester	сестра́	y tá
thermometer	termómetro	thermomètre	termometro	Thermometer	гра́дусник	nhiệt kế
stethoscope	estetoscopio	stéthoscope	stetoscopio	Hörrohr	стетоско́й	ống nghe
blood pressure gauge	válvula de tensión de sangre	sphygmomètre	sfigmomanometro	Blutdruckmesser	мано́метр	dụng cụ đo áp lực máu
syringe	jeringuilla	seringue	siringa	Spritze	шприц	ống chích
pills, medicine	píldoras, medicina	pilule, médicament	pillole, medicina	Medizin	табле́тки, лека́рство	viên thuốc, thuốc
doctor's bag	cartera del médico	sac de médecin	borsa da dottore	Arztasche	враче́бная су́мка	túi xách của bác sĩ
waiting room	recepción	salle d'attente	sala d'aspetto	Wartezimmer	ко́мната для посети́телей	phòng đợi
examining table	camilla	table d'auscultation	lettino da visite	Untersuchungstisch	стол для осмо́тра пацие́нтов	bàn khám bệnh
X-ray	rayos x	radiographie	raggi	Röntgenbild	рентге́н	quang tuyến
cast	escayola	plâtre	ingessatura	Gipsverband	ги́псовой слéпок	băng bột
operating room	sala de cirugía	salle d'opération	sala operatoria	Operationssaal	операцио́нная	phòng mổ
wheelchair	silla de ruedas	fauteuil roulant	sedia a rotelle	Rollstuhl	крéсло на колёсах	xe lăn
crutches	muletas	béquilles	stampelle	Krücken	костьли́	nạng
ambulance	ambulancia	ambulance	autoambulanza	Krankenwagen	ско́рая по́мощь	xe cứu thương

Vocabulary Supplement parts of the body, common illnesses

Teaching Suggestions

1. Point to the item and model the sentence for the students. Have them use the sentence to identify the pictures.
   This is a doctor. (nurse, thermometer, etc.)
   That is a doctor. (nurse, thermometer, etc.)
   Change to the plural.
   These are doctors. (nurses, etc.)
   Those are doctors. (nurses, etc.)
   Add an appropriate adjective.
   This is a tall doctor.   That is a glass thermometer.   These are new nurses.
   Those are silver stethoscopes.

2. Point to a picture and ask the following questions. Direct the students to answer in complete sentences.
   What is that?   What is this?   What are these?   What are those?

3. Complete the following with a logical answer.
   A _____ is a person who treats the sick. (doctor)
   A _____ assists the doctor. (nurse)
   A _____ measures a person's temperature. (thermometer)
   A _____ is used to listen to the heart and lungs. (stethoscope)

   A _____ measures the force of a heart pumping blood. (blood pressure gauge)
   A _____ is used to give a shot or injection. (syringe)
   _____ are prescribed to cure or prevent an illness. (pills, medicine)
   A doctor keeps instruments and some medicine in a _____. (doctor's bag)
   A patient waits to see a doctor in a _____. (waiting room)
   A doctor looks over a patient on an _____. (examining table)
   An _____ is a picture of a person's teeth or bones. (X-ray)
   A _____ is a plaster mold put on a broken bone to immobilize it. (cast)
   A doctor performs a surgical procedure in an _____. (operating room)
   A _____ assists a person who cannot walk. (wheelchair)
   A person with an injured leg can use _____ to aid in walking. (crutches)
   An _____ is a vehicle which transports sick or injured people. (ambulance)

Activities

1. Change the completion statements in Teaching Suggestions number 3 to question form. (Who assists a doctor?)
2. Play "What am I?" This game can be played spontaneously or you can have the students prepare it for a future class.
   I am made of glass.
   I have numbers printed on me.
   I have a red liquid inside.
   What am I?   (thermometer)
3. Direct the students to write the plural form of the words on the line provided.
4. Ask the students to give a suitable word or phrase in response to the vocabulary items. (doctor — hospital, etc.)
5. Using an imaginary or real telephone, have students call for an appointment with a doctor.
6. Set up a doctor's office in the classroom. Have one student be a doctor; another, a nurse; another, a patient. Suggest an ailment (sore throat, broken arm) for the patient to describe to the doctor and nurse. The doctor and nurse should "treat" the patient trying to use as many of the vocabulary words as possi-

ble. The other students can keep score of the words used.
7. What is the use or purpose of each item?
8. Are you afraid to visit a doctor? Why or why not? Why do you suppose some people are afraid?
9. Were you ever a patient in a hospital? Why?
10. Borrow a thermometer, stethoscope and/or a blood pressure gauge from the school nurse or health office. Show how they are used.
11. What do you do for a sore throat? Headache? Toothache? Cut? Scratch?
12. Would you want to be a doctor or a nurse? Why or why not?
13. What education does a person need to become a doctor or a nurse?
14. Have you ever had an X-ray taken? What for? Where? When?
15. What other occupations or jobs are related to a doctor and/or hospital? (orderly, laboratory technician, X-ray technician, receptionist, dietician, nurse's aide, practical nurse, etc.)

4. Post Office

Vocabulary

English	Spanish	French	German	Italian	Russian	Vietnamese
envelope	sobre	enveloppe	Briefumschlag	busta	конвѐрт	bao thơ
address	dirección	adresse	Adresse	indirizzo	áдрес	địa chỉ
return address	remite	adresse de l'expéditeur	Absender	mittente	обрáтный áдрес	địa chỉ người gửi
stamp	sello, estampilla	timbre	Briefmarke	francobollo	мáрка	tem
postmark	matasellos	timbre d'oblitération	Poststempel	timbro postale	почтóвый штéмпель	dấu bưu điện
letter	carta	lettre	Brief	lettera	письмó	thư
bill	cuenta, factura	facture	Rechnung	conto, avviso, fattura	счёт	giấy tính tiền
postcard	tarjeta postal	carte postale	Postkarte, Ansichtskarte	cartolina postale	почтóвая открытка	bưu thiếp
package, parcel	paquete	paquet	Paket	pacco postale	бандерóль, посылка	bưu kiện, gới đồ
string, twine	cuerda	ficelle	Bindfaden	spago	верёвка, шпагáт	dây cột hàng
scale	báscula	balance	Waage	bilancia	весы́	cân
stamp machine	distribuidor de sellos	distributeur de timbres	Briefmarkenautomat	apparecchio per francobolli	автомáт продáжи мáрок	máy đóng tem
post office box	apartado postal	boîte postale	Postfach	casella postale	—	hộp thư bưu điện
letter carrier	cartero	facteur	Briefträger	postino, portalettere	почтальóн	người đưa thư
mail truck	camión de correos	camion postal	Postwagen	vagone postale	почтóвая машина	xe thư
mailbox	buzón	boîte aux lettres	Briefkasten	cassetta postale	почтóвый ящик	thùng thư

Vocabulary Supplement parts of a letter, types of letters

Teaching Suggestions

1. Point to the item and model the sentence. Have students use it to identify the pictures.
There is an envelope. (address, etc.)
Change to the plural.
There are envelopes. (addresses, etc.)
Change the tense.
There was an envelope. (address, etc.)
2. Point to a picture and ask the following questions. Direct the students to answer in complete sentences.
What is there? What is this/that? What is to the left of the bill? What is below the right of the address? What is on top of the mail truck? What is next to the postcard?
3. Complete the following with a logical answer.
An ___ is a folded piece of paper which holds a letter. (envelope)
An ___ is the person, street number, and city to whom the mail is directed. (address)
A ___ is the address of the person who sent the letter. (return address)
A ___ is a small piece of paper glued on an envelope to pay its postage or delivery. (stamp)

A ___ records the time and place a letter passed through a post office. (postmark)
A ___ is a type of correspondence from one person to another. (letter)
A ___ is a written record of purchases, and it requests payment. (bill)
A ___ is a small card which has space for an address and a short note. (postcard)
A box wrapped to mail is a ___. (package)
___ is used to tie a package. (string)
Letters and packages are weighed on a ___ to determine the postage due. (scale)
One can insert coins into a ___ to buy stamps. (stamp machine)
Some people and businesses have their mail delivered to a ___. (post office box)
A ___ delivers the mail. (letter carrier)
A ___ is a vehicle used by a letter carrier to pick up and deliver the mail. (mail truck)
A person puts a letter into a ___ to mail it. (mailbox)

Activities

1. What is an envelope? (an address, a return address, etc.)
2. What do you do with a stamp? (package, stamp machine, etc.)
3. Do you receive any bills in the mail? From whom? What happens if you do not pay a bill?
4. What is a form letter? Have you ever received one?
5. Explain the proper way to wrap a package so that the contents are not damaged in shipment.
6. Play Bingo. Use the completion statements from Teaching Suggestions number 3 as clues; direct the students to cover the answers or draw an X through them. Mix them up as you read them as clues since they appear in order.
7. Explain the differences between a personal and business letter. Have the students write one of each.
8. Address an envelope.
9. Set up a post office in the classroom. Have the students play the parts of a clerk, a person buying stamps, a person mailing a package, a person mailing a letter.
10. What other functions does the post office perform? (change of address, passport application)
11. Does the post office serve the same purpose in every country? Who runs the post office? Is the mail service just as good in each country? Does it cost the same to mail a letter?
12. You are a post office box and through your window you see many people every day. Describe them to us.
13. You are a postcard. In words or pictures, describe what happens to you after you are dropped into a mailbox.
14. Change the completion sentences in Teaching Suggestions number 3 to questions and direct the students to write the answers on the line provided. (Who is a person who delivers the mail? – letter carrier)
15. Make postcards from paper and have the students send them to one another.
16. Using the sixteen pictures as cues, have the students make up a story.

5. Police and Fire

Vocabulary

English	Spanish	French	Italian	German	Russian	Vietnamese
police officer	policía	agent de police	poliziotto, vigile	Polizist	полицéйский	nhân viên cảnh sát
police, patrol car	coche patrulla	voiture de police	macchina della polizia	Polizeiwagen	полиция, полицéйская машина	xe canh sát, xe đi tuần
police station	comisaría de policía	commissariat de police	commissariato di polizia, questura	Polizeiwache	полицéйский учáсток	bót, đồn cảnh sát
jail, cell	cárcel, celda	prison, cellule	carcere, prigione	Gefängnis	тюрьмá, кáмера	nhà tù, phòng giam
gun	pistola	arme à feu	pistola, fucile	Feuerwaffe	револьвéр	súng
holster	pistolera	étui de revolver	fondina da sella	Pistolenhalfter	кобýра	bao súng
badge	chapa	plaque	distintivo	Abzeichen	значóк	phù hiệu
uniform	uniforme	uniforme	divisa	Uniform	фóрма	đồng phục
fire	incendio	feu, incendie	incendio	Feuer	пожáр	cháy, hỏa hoạn
fire fighter, fireman	bombero	pompier	pompiere	Feuerwehrmann	пожáрный	lính chữa lửa
fire truck	camión de bomberos	voiture des pompiers	carro dei pompieri	Feuerwehrwagen	пожáрная машина	xe chữa lửa
firehouse, station	estación de bomberos	poste de pompiers	caserma dei pompieri	Feuerwehr	пожáрное депó	trạm chữa lửa
ladder	escalera	échelle	scala a piuoli	Leiter	пожáрная лéстница	thang
hose	manguera	tuyau d'incendie	manichetta	Feuerschlauch	шланг	vòi nước
axe	hacha	hache	piccone, ascia	Axt	топóр	búa, rìu
oxygen mask	máscara de oxígeno	masque d'oxygène	maschera di ossigeno	Sauerstoffmaske	кислорóдная мáска	mặt nạ dưỡng khí

Vocabulary Supplement   police and fire emergencies

Teaching Suggestions

1. Point to the item and model the sentence for the students. Have them use the sentence to identify the pictures.
   I see a police officer. (police car, etc.)
   Change the subject.
   You (He, She, We, They) see a police car.
   Change the tense.
   I saw (will see) a police officer.
2. Point to a picture and ask the following questions. Direct the students to answer in complete sentences.
   Who do you see?   What does he see?
   What do you see?   Do you see a gun?
   Do they see a fire?   Does she see an axe?
   Did you see a police car?   they/a jail?
   Will you see a badge?   we/a fire truck?
3. Complete the sentences with a logical answer.
   A _____ enforces our laws. (police officer)
   A _____ is a vehicle for use by the police. (police, patrol car)
   The headquarters of the police officers is the _____. (police station)
   People who commit a crime are kept in a _____. (jail)
   A _____ is a weapon which shoots bullets. (gun)
   A _____ holds a gun. (holster)
   A _____ is a piece of metal stamped with a police officer's number. (badge)
   A _____ is special clothing a person wears which is associated with a job or occupation. (uniform)
   A _____ is something burning. (fire)
   A _____ puts out fires. (fire fighter)
   A _____ is a vehicle which carries the fire fighters and equipment to a fire. (fire truck)
   A _____ is a building in which the fire trucks are stored. (firehouse)
   A _____ aids a fire fighter in climbing to high places. (ladder)
   A _____ carries the water to put out a fire. (hose)
   An _____ is used to chop or cut down something in the fire fighter's way. (axe)
   An _____ is placed over the face of a fire fighter to supply fresh air. (oxygen mask)

Activities

1. What is a police officer? (police station, police car, etc.)
2. What does a police officer do? (fire fighter, hose, etc.)
3. What does a police officer's uniform consist of? A fire fighter's?
4. Have you ever been in a police car? A police station? What for?
5. Change the completion statements in Teaching Suggestions number 3 to questions. Direct the students to write the answers on the line provided.
6. Play "What/Who am I?"
   I am used at a fire.
   I am long and thin.
   I carry water.
   What am I? (hose)
7. When would you call the police? The fire department?
8. Using a play or imaginary telephone, have the students call the police to report a car accident or the fire department to report a fire. Direct them to include the necessary information (name, address, injuries, etc.).
9. Play "Add-ons." The teacher gives a statement and a student adds a word or phrase to the original sentence.
   Teacher: I see a police officer.
   Student 1: I see a police officer in a police car.
   Student 2: I see a police officer in a police car near the police station.
   Try to do all sixteen items. You may want to use the pictures as cues for the students.
10. A police officer stops you for a traffic violation. What do you say and do?
11. Draw a floor plan of your house or apartment. Devise two escape routes in case of a fire.
12. Would you make a good fire fighter? Why or why not?
13. What are the different types of police officers? (traffic, patrol, etc.) What do they do?
14. Explain the divisions of a police department and have the students find out which precinct they live in.
15. Do you know where the fire alarms are in your school? Do you have fire drills? How often?
16. Do you think guns should be banned except for police and military use?
17. Do you think being a police officer or a fire fighter is a dangerous occupation?

6. Mass Transportation

Vocabulary

English	Spanish	French	Italian	German	Russian	Vietnamese
bus	autobús	autobus, autocar	autobus, filobus, tram	Bus	автóбус	xe buýt
subway	metro	métro	metropolitana (sotterranea)	Untergrundbahn	метрó	xe điện ngầm
elevated train	tren (elevado)	train aérien	treno sopraelevato	Hochbahn	пóезд в метрó	xe điện chạy trên cao
train (commuter)	tren	train de banlieue	treno locale	Zug	пассажирский пóезд	xe lửa (tàu điện)
bus driver	conductor de autobús	chauffeur d'autobus	autista di filobus	Busfahrer	водитель автóбуса	tài xế xe buýt
engineer	mecánico	mécanicien	macchinista	Lokomotivführer	машинúст	người lái tàu điện
conductor	conductor (de tren)	contrôleur	conduttore	Schaffner	кондýктор	người thu vé
bus stop	parada de autobús	arrêt d'autobus	fermata filobus	Bushaltestelle	останóвка автóбуса	trạm xe buýt
train station	estación de tren	gare	stazione	Bahnhof	железнодорóжная стáнция	trạm xe lửa
ticket booth	ventanilla	guichet	sportello	Fahrkartenschalter	билéтная кácca	quầy bán vé
platform	plataforma	quai	marciapiede	Bahnsteig	платфóрма	bục đứng chờ xe lửa
coin box (fare)	taquilla	—	cassetta dei gettoni	Kasse	автомáт для размéна дéнег	hộp tiền (vé xe)
token	ficha	jeton	gettone	Marke	жетóн	vé xé bằng kim khí
turnstile	portillo	tourniquet	cancelletto girevole	Drehkreuz	турникéт	cửa xoay từng người vào hay ra
transfer	trasbordo	transfert	biglietto cumulativo	Umsteiger	переcáдочный билéт, переcáдка	phiếu dùng đổi xe
track	vía	voie (de chemin de fer)	binario	Gleis	рельсóвый путь	đường rầy xe điện

Vocabulary Supplement   schedule, route, arrival, departure

Teaching Suggestions

1. Point to the item and model the sentence for the students. Have them use the sentence to identify the pictures.
   This is the bus. (subway, elevated train, etc.) Change to the indefinite article.
   This is a bus. (subway, elevated train, etc.) Change to the plural.
   These are the buses. (subways, elevated trains, etc.)

2. Point to a picture and ask the following questions. Students answer in complete sentences. What is this?   What are these?   Is this an engineer?   Are these buses?

3. Complete the following with a logical answer.
   A _____ is a vehicle which travels on a street and carries many people. (bus)
   A _____ is a train which travels through an underground tunnel. (subway)
   An _____ is a train which travels on elevated tracks. (elevated train)
   A _____ carries many people to work and home again. (commuter train)
   An _____ operates a train. (engineer)
   A _____ collects the passengers' fares on a train. (conductor)
   A bus stops at a _____ to pick up passengers. (bus stop)
   A train stops at a _____ to pick up passengers. (train station)
   Passengers pay their train fare at a _____. (ticket booth)
   A passenger boards an elevated train from a _____. (platform)
   A _____ is a machine into which bus fare is dropped. (coin box)
   A _____ is a small piece of metal which is used for bus or subway fare. (token)
   After paying their fare, passengers walk through a _____. (turnstile)
   A _____ is a piece of paper which allows a passenger to board another bus without paying another fare. (transfer)
   A train travels on a _____. (track)

Activities

1. Do you ride a bus to school? A school bus or a public bus? What is the difference?
2. Does the city or town in which you live have a bus system? Is it reliable? What is the bus fare?
3. Have you ever been on a subway? An elevated train? Did you like it?
4. Have you ever been on a commuter train? Have you ever taken a train trip? If so, where to? Did you like it?
5. Change the completion statements from Teaching Suggestions number 3 to question form. Have the students write the answers on the line provided. (What do passengers walk through after paying their train fare?)
6. On the chalkboard scramble the letters of the vocabulary items. Have a contest to see which student can unscramble all of them first. Example: tttieookhbc — ticket booth.
7. Point out to the students that there are short- and long-distance bus companies. Would you like to take a bus trip? Why or why not? Are there any advantages in taking a bus rather than a train or an airplane?
8. Where do you purchase train tickets? Bus or subway tokens?
9. You are a bus driver with a full load of passengers. You are lost. What do you do or say?
10. Set up a train ticket booth in the classroom. Have students take turns being the ticket agent, a passenger buying a one-way ticket, a passenger buying a round-trip ticket, a passenger buying a month's pass.
11. You may want to bring in a bus schedule and draw a small portion of it on the chalkboard. This will provide practice in reading any type of schedule. If the class knows numbers and how to tell time, you can question them about arrival and departure times, length of trip from one stop to another, etc.

7. Airport

Vocabulary

English	Spanish	French	Italian	German	Russian	Vietnamese
airport	aeropuerto	aéroport	aeroporto	Flughafen	аэропорт	phi trường
airplane	avión	avion	aeroplano	Flugzeug	самолёт	máy bay
pilot	piloto	pilote	pilota	Pilot	пилот	phi công
flight attendant	aeromozo, azafata	steward, hôtesse de l'air	assistente di volo	Stewardess	стюардéсса	tiếp viên phi hành
passenger	pasajero	passager	passeggero	Passagier	пассажир	hành khách
terminal	terminal	terminus, aérogare	arrivi e partenze	Flughafengebäude	конéчный пункт	trạm đến
luggage, baggage	maletas, equipaje	bagages	bagagli	Gepäck	багáж	hành lý
ticket counter	ventanilla	guichet	sportello	Fahrkartenschalter	билéтный контрóль	quầy vé
ticket	billete	billet	biglietto	Fahrkarte	билéт	vé
metal detector	detector de metales	détecteur de métal	ditettore metalli	Metallsonde	металлúческий детéктор	máy khám vũ khí
gate boarding area	puerta, zona de abordar	porte d'embarquement	cancello	Ausgang	впускнáя зóна	cổng lên máy bay
control tower	torre de control	tour de contrôle	torre di controllo	Kontrollturm	контрóльная вышка	tháp kiểm soát không lưu
air traffic controller	controlador de tráfico	contrôleur aérien	controllore di traffico aereo	Fluglotse	авиадиспéтчер	kiểm soát viên phi hành
runway	pista	piste	pista di atterraggio	Rollbahn	взлётная полосá	phi đạo
to take off	despegar	décoller	decollare	abfliegen	взлетáть	cất cánh
to land	aterrizar	atterrir	atterrare	landen	приземляться	đáp xuống

Vocabulary Supplement   travel phrases (one-way, round trip, to check in, to board)

Teaching Suggestions

1. Point to the item and model the sentence for the students. Have them use the sentence to identify the pictures.
   I am looking at an airport. (airplane, etc.)
   You (He, She, We, They) are (is) looking at an airport. (airplane, pilot, etc.)
   Change the subject.
   I was (will be) looking at an airport.
   Change the tense.
2. Point to a picture and ask the following questions. Direct the students to answer in a complete sentence.
   What are you looking at?   What is he looking at?   What are they looking at?   Are you looking at an airplane?   Are they looking at a pilot?   Were you looking at a runway?
3. Complete the following with a logical answer.
   Airplanes take off and land at an _____. (airport)
   An _____ is a vehicle which flies. (airplane)
   A _____ flies an airplane. (pilot)
   A _____ assists people on an airplane. (flight attendant)
   A _____ pays to fly on a plane. (passenger)

A _____ is an airport building where passengers check in for flights. (terminal)
Travelers pack their clothes and belongings in _____. (luggage)
Travelers pay for their flights at a _____. (ticket counter)
A _____ is a piece of paper confirming payment for a flight. (ticket)
A _____ sounds an alarm when metal is passed through it. (metal detector)
The _____ is the place at which passengers get on an airplane. (gate)
The _____ is usually a tall building from which airplane traffic is directed. (control tower)
An _____ is a person who gives pilots clearance for take-off and landing. (air traffic controller)
A _____ is a concrete strip or road on which a plane takes off or lands. (runway)
An airplane _____ when it flies up into the sky. (takes off)
An airplane _____ when it descends from the sky. (lands)

Activities

1. Is there an airport in your town or city? What is its name? Is it busy? Have you been there?
2. Have you ever been on an airplane? How was your first flight? Were you afraid? Why (not)?
3. What kinds of airplanes are there?
4. Would you want to be a pilot? A flight attendant? Are there any advantages in working for an airline?
5. What other occupations are related to or associated with an airport? (Ticket clerk, reservation agent, skycap, baggage truck driver, cook, etc.)
6. Where can you buy a plane ticket?
7. Play Bingo. Use the completion statements from Teaching Suggestions number 3 as clues; the players cover up or draw an X through the answers.
8. What clothing and/or accessories would you pack in your luggage for a trip to a warm climate? A cold climate?
9. Set up a ticket counter in the classroom. One student can be a ticket agent; another can be a passenger purchasing a one-way ticket; another can be a passenger purchasing a round-trip ticket.
10. Make a tour booklet of an airport by cutting out the pictures and adding descriptions.
11. Set up a control tower in the classroom with an air traffic controller conversing with a pilot who is requesting permission to take off and/or land.
12. Your luggage is lost at the airport. What do you do?
13. Play "What/Who am I?" // I am a person. / I fly an airplane. / I help the passenger. / Who am I?   (flight attendant)
14. Set up an airport information booth in the classroom. Have students be the information booth attendant, passengers asking for Gate C, the baggage claim area, a restaurant, a washroom, etc.
15. You are the X-ray machine through which pass the passengers' purses and hand luggage. Describe what you see inside the following: a man's briefcase, a little girl's overnight case, a teenage boy's flight bag, and a woman's purse.
16. Which passengers must go through customs? Why? Who runs the customs department?

8. Car

Vocabulary

English	Spanish	French	Italian	German	Russian	Vietnamese
key	llave	clef	chiave	Schlüssel	ключ	chìa khóa
steering wheel	volante	volant	volante	Lenkrad	руль	bánh lái
rearview mirror	espejo retrovisor	rétroviseur	retrovisivo	Rückspiegel	зéркало заднего вида	gương chiếu hậu
seat belt	cinturón de seguridad	ceinture de sécurité	cintura di sicurezza	Sicherheitsgurt	пристяжнóй ремéнь	giây nịt an toàn
dashboard	panel de control	tableau de bord	cruscotto	Armaturenbrett	щитóк	bảng đồng hồ trong xe
gearshift	cambio de mando (marchas)	boîte de changement de vitesse	cambio a leva	Gangschaltung	корóбка переключéния передáч	cần sang số
pedals (brake and accelerator)	pedales (de frenos y de acelerador)	frein, accélérateur	pedali (freno e acceleratore)	Fusshebel (Brems-hebel, Gashebel)	педáли, тóрмоз и акселерáтор	bàn đạp (thắng và ga)
turn signal	intermitente	clignotant	indicatore di direzione	Winker	сигнáл поворóта	đèn báo đổi hướng
windshield	parabrisas	pare-brise	parabrezza	Windschutzscheibe	ветровóе стеклó	kính chắn gió
hood	capota	capot	cofano	Motorhaube	капóт	nắp
engine, motor	motor	moteur	motore	Motor	мотóр	máy
fender	parachoques	pare-chocs	parafango	Kotflügel	крылó	vè xe
trunk	portaequipaje	coffre	portabagagli	Kofferraum	багáжник	thùng xe
headlight	faro delantero	phare	faro anteriore	Scheinwerfer	передняя фáра	đèn trước
taillight	faro trasero	feu arrière	fanale posteriore	Schlusslicht	зáдняя фáра	đèn lái
license plate	matricula	plaque matricule	targa di registrazione	Nummernschild	номернóй знак	bảng số xe

Vocabulary Supplement   additional parts of cars, types of cars

Teaching Suggestions

1. Point to the item and model the sentence for the students. Have them use the sentence to identify the pictures.

My car has a key. (hood, etc.)
Change the possessive.
Her (His, Your) car has a key. (hood, etc.)
Our (Their) car has a key. (hood, etc.)
Change to the plural.
My (Your, His, etc.) cars have a key.

2. Point to a picture and ask the following questions. Direct the students to answer in complete sentences.

What does my (his, your, our, their) car have?   Do his (our) cars have a turn signal?   Do our cars have headlights?

3. Complete the following with a logical answer.

A _____ unlocks a door. (key)
A _____ turns a vehicle's wheels. (steering wheel)
A driver can see what is behind through the _____. (rearview mirror)
A _____ straps and secures a person into a seat. (seat belt)
The _____ displays the car's gauges. (dashboard)

The _____ changes the gears of the car's transmission. (gearshift)
A driver presses the foot _____ to stop or to drive the car. (pedals)
A _____ indicates in which direction a car is going to turn. (turn signal)
The _____ is a piece of glass in front of the car through which the driver sees. (windshield)
The _____ covers the engine and other car parts. (hood)
The _____ is a machine which gives a car power to move. (engine)
The _____ covers the wheels and tires of a car. (fender)
The _____ is a compartment in the rear of the car which can be used for storage. (trunk)
A _____ provides light in front of a car. (headlight)
A _____ indicates that a car's headlights are on or that the car is stopping. (taillight)
A _____ is a metal plate with numbers to show the car is registered. (license plate)

Activities

1. Do you have a car? Does someone in your family have a car? What kind is it? What year is it? What color is it? Do you have a garage?

2. Do you know how to drive a car? When did you learn? Who taught you how to drive? Are you a good or careful driver?

3. Change the completion statements in Teaching Suggestions number 3 to questions. Direct the students to write the answers on the line provided. (What straps and secures a person into a seat? seat belt)

4. Alphabetize the vocabulary words.

5. What does a key do? (a steering wheel, rearview mirror, etc.)

6. What are the requirements for driving a car in the state in which you live? In Germany? In Italy? In France? In Spain?

7. Bring in a toy car or ask a student to draw a car on the chalkboard. Have the students take turns naming the parts of a car.

8. Set up a gas station in the classroom. One student can be the attendant, others can buy gas, ask directions, ask for an oil change, have their tires checked, or a bulb replaced in a headlight or a taillight.

9. Direct the students to draw an X through the items which are found inside a car. Direct them to circle the items which are in front of a car. Direct them to draw a T through the items which are in the rear of a car.

10. What are the different types of models of cars? (full-size, intermediate, compact, two-door, four-door, convertible, hatch-back, station wagon, etc.) What are the differences among them?

11. What would you do if you locked your key in the car?

12. You have just invented the automobile. Convince us it is a useful vehicle.

13. Set up a car dealership in the classroom. One student can be the salesperson, others can be buyers. Have the students include the following: model, year, color choices, optional equipment, automatic or manual transmission, gas mileage, price, type of tires, etc.

14. A car is a part of many jobs or occupations. Name some. (taxi driver, salesperson, police, etc.)

9. Road Signs

Vocabulary

English	Spanish	French	Italian	German	Russian	Vietnamese
stop	parar ("stop")	stop	stop	Halt	стоп	ngừng
yield	ceder el paso	signal de priorité	dare la precedenza	Vorfahrt gewähren	уступить	nhường
no U-turn	no retorno	Défense de faire demi-tour	vietata la conversione a U	nicht wenden	разворóт запрещён	cẩm queọ chữ U
left turn prohibited	prohibido girar a la izquierda	Défense de tourner à gauche	vietato girare a sinistra	vorgeschriebene Fahrtrichtung nach rechts	лéвый поворóт запрещён	cẩm queọ trái
do not enter	no entrar	Défense d'entrer	divieto di accesso	Einfahrtsverbot	въезд запрещён	cẩm vào
school	escuela	école	scuola	Schule	школа	trường học
begin divided highway	carretera dividida empieza	route nationale	—	Anfang der Autobahn	начáло двустороннего движéния	xa lộ bắt đầu chia làn
slippery when wet	resbaladizo cuando mojado	Chaussée glissante	sdrucciolevole quando è bagnato	Schleudergefahr	скóльзкая дорóга	trơn khi ướt
railroad crossing	vía ferrocarril	passage à niveau	passaggio a livello	Bahnübergang	железнодорóжный переéзд	chỗ cắt đường rầy
right turn ahead	vuelta a la derecha	virage à droite	girare a destra	vorn nach rechts biegen	впередú поворóт напрáво	queọ phải phía trước
crossroad	cruce de carretera	carrefour	crocevia	Kreuzung	перекрёсток	ngã tư
interstate	autopista	autoroute	autostrada	Autobahn	шоссé	giữã các tiểu bang
telephone	teléfono	téléphone	telefono	Telefon	телефóн	điện thoại
bike route	ruta de bicicleta	piste cyclable	corsia per biciclette	Radfahrerweg	велосипéдная дорóжка	đường xe đạp
lane ends, narrows	vía termina	voie étroite	fine della corsia	Ende, Engpass	сужéние дорóги	ngõ cụt, hẹp
winding road	carretera curvilínea	route sinueuse	strada tortuosa	kurvenreiche Strecke	извúлистая дорóга	đường ngoằn ngoèo

Vocabulary Supplement   shapes and colors of road signs

Teaching Suggestions

1. Point to the item and model the sentence for the students.
   This (that) is a stop sign. (yield. etc.)
2. Point to a picture and ask these questions.
   What is this/that/these/those?
   What is on top of/to the right/left of/below the stop sign?
3. Complete the following with a logical answer.
   An eight-sided sign means _____. (stop)
   A triangular-shaped sign always means _____. You must slow down or stop for other traffic. (yield)
   A red circle with a slash through it always means "NO." It says what is prohibited.
   This one means _____. (No U-Turn)
   This red circle with a slash means _____. (left turn prohibited)
   A red circle with a horizontal bar means _____. (do not enter)
   A _____ sign gives advance warning of a school building or crossing. (school)

This warning sign indicates a _____. (divided highway begins)
This sign says the road is _____ and speed should be reduced. (slippery when wet) The _____.
This sign warns that a _____ is near. The driver should look out for trains. (railroad crossing)
This sign warns a driver of a change in the road direction. This sign warns of a _____. (right turn ahead)
This sign warns that a _____ is ahead. Other cars may enter. (crossroad)
A shield-shaped sign indicates an _____. (interstate)
A square-shaped sign with a symbol is a _____ service sign. The service which is indicated on this sign is a _____. (telephone)
This sign indicates that the road is a _____. (bike route)
This sign says a _____. (lane ends, narrows)
This _____ sign warns a driver that a series of curves is ahead. (winding road)

Activities

1. What is a stop sign? A yield sign? A school crossing sign? Continue with all the signs.
2. List the different shapes and colors of the road signs. Your state's rules of the road can give you the information.
3. What do you do if you are driving a car and you see a school sign? A railroad crossing sign?
4. Draw a map which incorporates all the road signs listed.
5. Are traffic laws or regulations necessary? Why or why not?
6. Are these road signs used in Germany? In Spain? In Italy?
7. In the town or city in which you live, what are the fines for a parking violation or for running a stop sign? What is done with the money?
8. You are a police officer and have just stopped a car for an illegal left turn. Tell us your conversation with the driver.
9. Have a contest to see who can list or name additional road signs.
10. Do you have to take a test on these signs in the state in which you live in order to obtain a driver's license?

10. Street

Vocabulary

English	Spanish	French	Italian	German	Russian	Vietnamese
street, avenue	calle, avenida	rue, avenue	strada, via	Strasse	улица	đường phố, đại lộ
sidewalk	acera	trottoir	marciapiede	Bürgersteig	тротуáр	lề đường đi bộ
curb	cuneta	bord du trottoir	curva	Strassenkante	обóчина	bờ lề
traffic light	semáforo	feu	semaforo	Verkehrsampel	светофóр	đèn lưu thông
crosswalk	cruce (de peatones)	passage piétonnier	passaggio pedonale	Zebrastreifen	перехóд	lối đi bộ băng qua đường
pedestrian	peatón	piéton	pedoni	Fussgänger	пешехóд	người đi bộ
corner	esquina	coin	angolo	Ecke	угол	góc đường
streetlight	luz (de la calle)	réverbère	luce stradale	Strassenlaterne	уличный фонáрь	đèn đường
fire hydrant	bomba de agua	bouche d'incendie	idrante	Feuerhahn	пожáрный кран	vòi nước chửa lửa
parking meter	parquímetro	parcomètre	contatore per parcheggio	Parkuhr	счётчик	cột trả tiền đậu xe
litter, trash can	cubo de basura	poubelle	pattumiera	Abfalleimer	урна для мýсора	rác, thùng rác
emergency telephone	teléfono de emergencia	téléphone de police-secours	telefono di emergenza	Notfernsprecher	телефóн скóрой пóмощи	điện thoại khẩn cấp
newsstand, kiosk	quiosco	kiosque à journaux	edicola	Kiosk	газéтный киóск	quán, sap báo
street sign	señal de la calle	poteau indicateur	segnale stradale	Strassenzeichen	уличный знак	dấu hiệu đi đường
neon sign	señal de neón	enseigne au néon	luci al neon	Neonlicht	неóновый знак	đèn quảng cáo
manhole, sewer	cloaca	égout	botola, pozzetto	Mannloch, Abwasserkanal	люк канализáции	cống, cống nước

Vocabulary Supplement   types of buildings, stores, shops

Teaching Suggestions

1. Point to the item and model the sentence for the students. Have them use the sentence to identify the pictures.
   I see a street. (sidewalk, curb, etc.)
   Change the subject.
   You/He see(s) a street (curb, etc.).
   Change the tense.
   She/they will see (saw) a street.
2. Point to a picture and ask the following questions. Direct the students to answer in complete sentences.
   What do you (he, etc.) see?   Did (Will) you see a curb?
3. Complete the following with a logical answer.
   A _____ is a public road. (street)
   People walk on a _____. (sidewalk)
   A _____ is the edge of a street. (curb)
   A _____ indicates when cars are to stop or go. (traffic light)
   People should cross a street at a _____. (crosswalk)
   A _____ is a person who is walking. (pedestrian)
   A _____ is where two streets meet. (corner)
   A _____ illuminates or brightens an area at night. (streetlight)

   A _____ is an above-ground pipe from which water is drawn to put out a fire. (fire hydrant)
   A _____ is a machine into which a driver puts coins to pay for the use of a parking space. (parking meter)
   A _____ is a container used to hold discarded or thrown-away papers. (litter can)
   An _____ is used to contact the police or fire department. (emergency telephone)
   Newpapers and magazines are sold at a _____. (newsstand)
   A _____ gives the name of a street. (street sign)
   A _____ is used to give information about a store, shop, or other place of business. (neon sign)
   A _____ is a covered hole in the street through which one can reach a sewer. (manhole)

Activities

1. Do you cross a street at a crosswalk? Does your town or city have a jay-walking law? If so, is it enforced?
2. Have you ever used an emergency telephone? Why? Do you have to insert money in order to place the call?
3. Do you walk by trash on the sidewalk or do you pick it up and throw it in a litter can?
4. Play "What/Who am I?"
   I am usually painted red.
   I am made of metal.
   I am full of water.
   What am I?   (fire hydrant)
5. Play "Add-ons".
   Teacher: I see a street.
   Student 1: I see a street and a sidewalk.
   Student 2: I see a street and a sidewalk with a curb.
   Continue until all the vocabulary items are used. You may want to cue the students by pointing to the pictures.
6. Change the completion statements in Teaching Suggestions number 3 to question form. Direct the students to write the answers on the line provided.
7. Have the students draw a street on a piece of paper or the chalkboard. Ask different students to draw a vocabulary item on the street.
8. You have parked your car but the parking meter is broken. What do you do?
9. You are a litter can (emergency phone, a fire hydrant, etc.). Tell us your life story. Include your best and worst moments.
10. Take an alien from outer space for a walk down a street. Explain what you see using as many vocabulary items as possible.
11. What kinds of stores are there on a street in the town or city in which you live? What can you buy in them?
12. Ask the students to give you a word related to or associated with each of the vocabulary items. (fire hydrant — water, sidewalk — cement)
13. Design a neon sign for a store or restaurant of your choice.

11. Occupations

Vocabulary

English	Spanish	French	Italian	German	Russian	Vietnamese
architect	arquitecto	architecte	architetto	Architekt	архитéктор	kiến trúc sư
house painter	pintor	peintre en bâtiment	pittore	Anstreicher	маляр	người sơn nhà
watchman	guarda	garde	guardia	Wächter	ночнóй стóрож	người canh gác
custodian, janitor	barrendero	concierge	portinaio	Hausmeister	двóрник	người bảo trì, gác dan
photographer	fotógrafo	photographe	fotografo	Photograph	фотóграф	thợ chụp hình
journalist, reporter	periodista	journaliste	giornalista, riporter	Journalist, Berichterstatter	журналíст, репортёр	nhà báo, phóng viên
pharmacist	farmacéutico	pharmacien, -enne	farmacista	Apotheker, Drogist	фармацéвт	dược sĩ
librarian	bibliotecario	bibliothécaire	bibliotecario	Bibliothekar	библиотéкарь	người quản thủ thư viện
hair stylist	peluquero	coiffeur, coiffeuse	parrucchiere	Friseur, Friseuse	парикмáхер	thợ làm tóc
computer programmer, operator	operador de computadora	programmeur d'ordinateur	programmatore di computer	Programmierer/ Programmiererin	оперáтор-программíст	người viết chương trình, điều hành máy điện tử
veterinarian	veterinario	vétérinaire	veterinario	Tierarzt	ветеринáр	thú y sĩ
paramedic	practicante	auxiliaire médical	paramedico	ärztlicher Beistand	рабóтник скóрой пóмощи	trợ y
factory worker	trabajador (de fábrica)	ouvrier, -ière d'usine	lavoratore	Fabrikarbeiter	рабóчий	thợ xưởng
office worker	oficinista	employé(e) de bureau	impiegato	Büroarbeiter	служащий	nhân viên văn phòng
disc jockey	disc jockey	animateur, -trice, de radio	annunciatore radio-fonico	Rundfunkansager	музыкáльный рабóтник рáдио	Xướng ngôn viên
repairman, person	reparador	réparateur	tecnico	Handwerker	ремóнтный рабóчий	thợ sửa chữa

Vocabulary Supplement   work related to the occupations, equipment

Teaching Suggestions

1. Point to the item and model the sentence for the students. Have them use the sentence to identify the pictures.

   I am an architect. (house painter, etc.)
   Change the subject.
   He (You, etc.) is (are) an architect(s).
   Change the tense.
   He (She, etc.) will be (was) an architect(s).

2. Point to a picture and ask the following questions. Direct the students to answer in complete sentences.
   What are you/they?   What is he?
   Is she a reporter?   Is he a watchman?
   Is he going to be a paramedic?

3. Complete the following with a logical answer.
   An _____ draws plans for a new building. (architect)
   A _____ paints the walls of a house. (house painter)
   A _____ guards a building. (watchman)
   A _____ fixes broken items in a building. (custodian)

   A _____ takes pictures. (photographer)
   A _____ reports the news. (journalist)
   A _____ prepares medicine. (pharmacist)
   A _____ checks books in and out of a library. (librarian)
   A _____ cuts and/or curls hair. (hair stylist)
   A _____ writes codes or instructions for a computer. (computer programmer)
   A _____ is a doctor for animals. (veterinarian)
   A _____ assists a doctor or a nurse or is a person who aids an emergency or accident victim. (paramedic)
   A _____ is a person who works in a building in which something is made or built. (factory worker)
   An _____ is a person who performs duties or services in an office. (office worker)
   A _____ is a radio announcer who plays and comments on records. (disc jockey)
   A _____ fixes broken items, such as a washing machine or a television set. (repairman)

Activities

1. What does a watchman do? An architect? A paramedic? Continue with all occupations.
2. Do you know a veterinarian/librarian, etc.?
3. What does a veterinarian need to do his job? (an animal, instruments, medicine, X-ray machine, bandages, etc.) Continue with all.
4. Play Bingo. Read the completion statements from Teaching Suggestions number 3 as clues; the players cover up or draw an X through the answer.
5. Where does an architect work? A house painter? A hair stylist? Continue occupations.
6. Would you like to be a watchman? Why (not)?
7. Is any special education needed to be an architect? A hair stylist? Continue with all the occupations. Your school library probably has a book which lists the education needed for the occupations listed.
8. Do any of these occupations require a license to practice? Who issues the license? What do you have to do in order to receive one?
9. You are a television reporter interviewing a paramedic (pharmacist, architect, etc.). Ask the paramedic to describe a typical day but get some background information also (on-the-job training, what made the person decide on this occupation).
10. Play "Who am I?"
    I sit at a desk. I work in a building. I handle many books during the day. (librarian)
11. Have the students find out the meaning of the following: employment agency, reference, résumé, employee, employer, self-employed, full-time, part-time, shared time, benefits, health and dental insurance, sick days, vacation days, personnel department.
12. Bring in some help wanted ads. If necessary, explain them to the students. Have the students write a help wanted ad for one of the occupations listed.
13. Direct the students to write their own résumés.
14. Set up an employment agency in the classroom. Students play interviewer - applicant.
15. Are any of these occupations dangerous? Exciting? Helpful?

12. Shopping

Vocabulary

English	Spanish	French	Italian	German	Russian	Vietnamese
shopping cart	carrito	chariot	carrello	Einkaufswagen	тележка	lối vào, phòng khách
cash register	caja	caisse	cassa	Kasse	кассовый аппарáт	chỗ trả tiền
sales receipt	recibo	reçu	ricevuta di vendita	Quittung	кассовый чек	biên lai bán hàng
credit card machine	máquina de tarjetas de crédito	machine pour cartes de crédit	macchinetta per carte di credito	Kredikarten-Maschine	кредитно-кáрточная машина	máy trả tiền lối tín dụng
paper bag, sack	bolsa	sac en papier	sacchetto	Tüte	бумáжный мешóк	túi, xách giấy
price tag	etiqueta de precio	étiquette, prix	etichetta del prezzo	Preiszettel	этикéтка	mẫu ghi giá hàng
size tag	etiqueta de talla	étiquette, taille	etichetta misura	Grössenzettel	ярлык	mẫu ghi kích thước
display case	mostrador	vitrine	vetrina	Schaukasten	витрина прилáвка	quầy trưng hàng
counter	mostrador	comptoir	banco	Ladentisch	прилáвок	quầy
rack	estante	rayon	attaccapanni	Stange	вéшалка	kệ
escalator	escaleras giratorias	escalier roulant	scala mobile	Rolltreppe	эскалáтор	thang cuốn
elevator	ascensor, elevador	ascenseur	ascensore	Lift, Aufzug	лифт	thang máy
fitting room	cuarto de pruebas	cabine d'essayage	stanzino di prova	Umkleidekabine	примéрочная	phòng thử quần áo
customer service desk, booth	puesto de servicio al cliente	bureau du chef de service	banco di assistenza ai clienti	Kundendienst	прилáвок для обслýживания покупáтелей, кабина	quầy phục vụ khách hàng
advertisement	anuncio	réclame, publicité	reclam	Anzeige	объявлéние	quảng cáo
sales clerk	dependiente	vendeur, vendeuse	commesso, -a	Verkäufer	продавéц	nhân viên bán hàng

Vocabulary Supplement   sections in a grocery and department store

Teaching Suggestions

1. Point to item and model sentence for students; have them use it to identify pictures.
   I am looking for a shopping cart (etc.). Change the subject./Change the tense.
2. Point to a picture and ask the following questions. Direct the students to answer in complete sentences.
   What are you (we, they, he) looking for? Were you (they, etc.) looking for a shopping cart? Will you (he, etc.) be looking for a sales clerk?
3. Complete the following with a logical answer.
   I put the food I want to buy in a _____. (shopping cart)
   The store clerk puts money into the _____. (cash register)
   A _____ is a listing of what I bought and how much it cost. (sales receipt)
   A _____ stamps a credit card onto a sales receipt. (credit card machine)
   The items one buys are placed in a _____. (paper bag)
   A _____ is attached to an item to tell us how much it costs. (price tag)
   A _____ is attached to an article of clothing to tell us what size it is. (size tag)

A _____ is a cabinet in which items to be bought are shown or displayed. (display case)
A _____ is the top surface of a cabinet or display case. (counter)
A _____ is a stand on which items, such as clothing, are hung. (rack)
An _____ is a moving stairway. (escalator)
An _____ is a machine which moves people or things up and down. (elevator)
A _____ is a small cubicle or room in which a buyer can try on clothes. (fitting room)
A _____ has a clerk who assists a buyer in returning items or correcting bills. (customer service desk)
An _____ is a notice of a sale or promotion in a store. (advertisement)
A _____ helps the buyer. (sales clerk)

Activities

1. Do you like to go shopping? Why? What for?
2. Circle the pictures you would see in a grocery store; draw an X through the pictures you would see in a department store.
3. Set up a grocery store check-out line in the classroom. Have students take turns being the clerk and customers. You can use newspaper or magazine pictures for the products and a toy cash register or even a calculator to ring up the sale.
4. What do you find in the produce section of a grocery store? The dairy section? Frozen food section? Delicatessen? Canned goods section? Paper products section? Try to elicit specific products as answers.
5. In what section of a department store would you find socks? Cribs? An electric saw? Blouses? Boots? Radios? Lipstick? A bracelet?
6. You are a salesperson in the clothing section of a department store. Show your customer the selection of women's blouses (men's shirts). The customer can ask the price, size, material, care, where the fitting room is, etc.
7. Discuss the different methods of payment — cash, check, store charge card, bank credit card, C.O.D. (cash on delivery), lay-away.
8. Draw a section or floor of a department store. Include as many of the vocabulary items as possible.
9. Make up a grocery list for a meal you are planning. Include a salad, meat, vegetable, potato, and dessert. Find out from a newspaper ad how much your meal will cost.
10. The cash register has just given you a total you know is incorrect! What do you do?
11. Have you ever been stuck in an elevator? For how long? How did you get out?
12. Write an advertisement for your favorite food, article of clothing, car, book, record, or movie.

13. Office

Vocabulary

English	Spanish	French	Italian	German	Russian	Vietnamese
desk	escritorio	bureau	scrivania	Schreibtisch	письменный стол	bàn giấy
typewriter	máquina de escribir	machine à écrire	macchina da scrivere	Schreibmaschine	пишущая машинка	máy đánh chữ
file cabinet	archivo	classeur	classificatore	Aktenkasten	картотека	tủ giấy tờ
copy machine	copiadora	photocopieur	macchina fotostatica	Kopierer	копировальная машина	máy chụp giấy tờ
dictaphone	dictáfono	dictaphone	dittofono	Diktiergerät	диктофон	máy thu băng và đọc lại cho người khác ghi lại
calculator	calculadora	calculatrice	calcolatore, calcolatrice	Taschenrechner	калькулятор	máy tính máy cộng
adding machine	máquina sumadora	machine à calculer	calcolatore	Rechenmaschine	счётная машина	
water cooler	fuente, alcarraza	alcarazas	refrigeratore d'acqua	Wasserkühler	водоохладитель	bình nước uống cấp
briefcase	cartera	serviette	cartella	Aktentasche	портфёль	cái đóng sách
stapler	grapadora	agrafeuse	cucitrice per graffette	Hefter	скрепйтель для бумáг	băng đính
cellophane tape	cinta adhesiva	scotch	nastro adesivo	Tesafilm	целлофáновая плёнка	dao mở thư
letter opener	abrecartas	coupe-papier	tagliacarte	Brieföffner	открывáтель для писем	cái kẹp giấy
paper clip	sujetapapeles	trombone	fermacarte	Briefklammer	скрéпка	giấy thun
rubber band	gomita	élastique	elastico	Gummiband	клеющая лéнта	
time clock	reloj	horloge enregis-treuse, pointeuse	orologio di controllo, marcatempo	Stechuhr	часы́-тáбель	đồng hồ bấm giờ
time card	tarjeta de tiempo	carte de pointage	cartellino di tempo	Stempelkarte	тáбель	thẻ bấm giờ

Vocabulary Supplement
office functions or jobs

Teaching Suggestions

1. Point to the item and model the sentence for the students. Have them use the sentence to identify the pictures.
   This is my desk. (typewriter, etc.)
   Change the possessive.
   This is his (her) desk. (typewriter, etc.).
   Change to the plural.
   These are my (your) desks (typewriters, etc.).
2. Point to a picture and ask the following questions. Direct the students to answer in complete sentences.
   Is this my desk?   Is this her typewriter?
   Is this his briefcase?   Is this our stapler?
3. Complete the following with a logical answer.
   I sit on a chair at my _____. (desk)
   I write letters on my _____. (typewriter)
   I store papers in a _____. (file cabinet)
   I make duplicates of my papers on a _____. (copy machine)
   I record my letters or memos on a _____. (dictaphone)

I do my mathematics assignments on a _____. (calculator)
A machine which finds sums and totals is an _____. (adding machine)
I drink water from a _____. (water cooler)
I put my papers into a _____ to carry them home. (briefcase)
A _____ is a device which attaches a small piece of wire to pieces of paper to hold them together. (stapler)
I use _____ to fix a ripped or torn piece of paper. (cellophane tape)
A _____ opens envelopes. (letter opener)
A _____ is a bent piece of metal which hold papers together. (paper clip)
A _____ is made from elasticized rubber and holds things together. (rubber band)
An employee checks or punches in and out of work on a _____. (time clock)
An employee inserts a _____ into a time clock to record time worked. (time card)

Activities

1. What is the function or purpose of each item?
2. Is there a difference between an adding machine and a calculator?
3. Play Bingo. Read the completion statements from Teaching Suggestions number 3 as clues; direct the students to cover up or draw an X through the answers. To determine one winner, ask the players to give a definition of the words or to spell them.
4. Circle the items you would find in a desk. Draw an X through the items you would find on a desk.
5. On the chalkboard scramble the letters of each of the vocabulary items. Have a contest to see which student can unscramble them first. Direct the students to write the correct word on each line provided.
   Example: keds (desk)
   neptteeelrro (letter opener)
6. Have the students draw an office or cut pictures from a magazine or catalogue. Use all the vocabulary items in the drawing.
7. You are an office desk. Describe your day.
8. How many types of offices can you think of? Describe what is done in each. (doctor's office, school office, etc.)
9. You are an office manager. Explain each item to a recently hired person.
10. Would you like to work in an office? Why (not)?
11. Invite a member of the business education department to visit your class to explain the skills needed to work in an office.
12. Is a typewriter in an office in Madrid or Berlin the same as one used in Chicago or New York?
13. Name or list the occupations which would use the following: typewriter, file cabinet, copy machine, dictating machine, adding machine, calculator. (typewriter — secretary, author, reporter, typist, billing clerk, etc.)

14. Restaurant

Vocabulary

English	Spanish	French	Italian	German	Russian	Vietnamese
waiter, waitress	camarero, -a mozo, -a	garçon, serveuse	cameriere, cameriera	Kellner, Kellnerin	официант, официантка	cậu, cô bồi bàn
chef, cook	cocinero	chef de cuisine	cuoco	Koch	шеф-повар	người nấu ăn
entrance	entrada	entrée, porte d'entrée	entrata	Eingang	вход	lối vào
exit	salida	sortie	uscita	Ausgang	выход	lối ra
menu	carta	carte	menu	Speisekarte	меню	thực đơn
check, bill	cuenta, nota	addition	conto	Rechnung	чек, счёт	phiếu tính tiền, hóa đơn
cashier	cajero	caissier, caissière	cassiere	Kassierer	кассир	người thu tiền
checkroom, cloakroom	guardarropa	vestiaire	guardaroba	Garderobe	гардеробная	phòng gởi áo
tray	bandeja	plateau	vassoio	Tablett	поднос	khay
placemat	(mantel) individual	napperon individuel	tovaglietta all'americana	Set	поднос с прибором	miếng phủ bàn ăn cho mỗi người
salad	ensalada	salade	insalata	Salat	салат	món rau trộn
main course, entrée	plato principal	plat principal	primo piatto	Hauptgericht	пёрвое блюдо	món ăn chính
dessert	postre	dessert	dolci e frutta	Nachtisch	десёрт	món tráng miệng
counter	mostrador	comptoir	banco	Theke	прилавок	quầy
table	mesa	table	tavolo	Tisch	стол	bàn
booth	—	—	—	Ecktisch	кабина	bàn ăn ở góc, cạnh tường

Vocabulary Supplement food

Teaching Suggestions

1. Point to the item and model the sentence for the students. Have them use the sentence to identify the pictures.
   I want a waiter/waitress. (salad, etc.)
   Add a possessive
   I want my waiter/waitress. (salad, etc.)
   Change the subject and possessive.
   She (He, You, We, They) wants (want) her (his, your, our, their) waiter/waitress.
2. Point to a picture and ask the following questions. Direct the students to answer in complete sentences.
   What do you (they, etc.) want? Does he want your salad/my dessert?
3. Complete the following with a logical answer.
   A _____ serves a meal in a restaurant. (waiter/waitress)
   A _____ prepares restaurant food. (chef)
   I go into a restaurant through the _____. (entrance)
   I leave through the _____. (exit)
   A _____ lists the food served and its price. (menu)
   A _____ is a list of the cost of the food usually given to the diner at the end of the meal. (check)
   A _____ takes money in a restaurant. (cashier)
   In a restaurant I hang my jacket in the _____. (cloakroom)
   The waiter brings food to a table on a _____. (tray)
   A _____ is a covering spread over the dining table before the places are set. (placemat)
   A _____ is a mixture of raw vegetables served with a dressing. (salad)
   A _____ is usually eaten after the dessert. (main course)
   _____ is usually a sweet food served at the end of a meal. (dessert)
   A _____ is a long flat surface at which many people can sit to be served. (counter)
   A _____ is a piece of furniture at which people sit to eat. (table)
   A _____ has a table and seats whose backs act as partitions. (booth)

Activities

1. Change the completion statements from Teaching Suggestions number 3 to true and false. (A cook serves me my meal in a restaurant.)
2. Change the completion statements from Teaching Suggestions number 3 to question form. Direct the students to write the answer on the line provided. (What lists the food served and its price?)
3. Circle what you can eat. Draw an X through what can talk.
4. Play "Add-ons."
   Teacher: I see a restaurant.
   Student 1: I see a restaurant with a waitress.
   Student 2: I see a restaurant with a waitress and a chef.
   Continue with all the vocabulary items.
5. Set up a restaurant in the classroom. Have the students take turns being a waiter/waitress, chef, customer, and cashier. Direct them to include entering, being seated with a choice of a table, booth, counter; requesting the menu, ordering a salad, main course, dessert, paying, tipping, and leaving.
6. What do you like to eat in a salad? What kind of dressing do you like? What is your favorite dessert? What is your favorite meal?
7. What is your favorite restaurant? Why? Do you eat there often?
8. What kinds or types of restaurants are there in your neighborhood? What do they specialize in?
9. What are the different types of restaurants? (fast food, take out, café, coffee shop, deli, ethnic, etc.)
10. You are a waiter or a waitress and your customer cannot decide what to order. What do you say to help?
11. You are a restaurant manager hiring for the positions of chef, waiter, waitress, and cashier. Interview the applicants.
12. Does a restaurant need a license to operate? Why? Who issues the license?

15. Food

Vocabulary

English	Spanish	French	Italian	German	Russian	Vietnamese
pizza	pizza	pizza	pizza	Pizza	пицца	món pizza
chips (potato)	patatas fritas (a la inglesa)	(pommes) chips	patatine fritte	Chips	жáреный картóфель	lát khoai tây chiên
french fries	patatas fritas	pommes frites	patate fritte	Pommes frites	жáреный картóфель по-францýзски	khoai tây chiên
popcorn	palomitas	popcorn	"popcorn"	Popcorn	воздýшная кукурýза	bắp rang
candy bar	pastilla de chocolate	tablette de chocolat	cioccolato	Tafel Schokolade	конфéты	thanh kẹo
chewing gum	chicle	chewing gum	gomma da masticare	Kaugummi	жевáтельная резúнка	kẹo cao su
lollipop	chupachús	sucette	lecca-lecca	Lutscher	леденéц	kẹo quế
catsup	salsa de tomate	ketchup	"catsup"	Tomatenketschup	кéтчуп	tương cà chua
mustard	mostaza	moutarde	senape	Senf	горчúца	mù tạc
rolls, buns	panecillos	petits pains	panini	Brötchen	слáдкие бýлочки	bánh mì mềm
doughnut	bollito	beignet	ciambella	Berliner	пышка	bánh ngọt đơn nất
cupcake	tartita	–	pasticcino	Teilchen	кекс	bánh ngọt nhỏ
beer	cerveza	bière	birra	Bier	пúво	la ve
wine	vino	vin	vino	Wein	винó	rượu chất
soft drink	refresco	boisson carbonisée	bibita	alkoholfreies Getränk	лёгкий напúток	nước ngọt
milkshake	batido	milkshake	frullato di latte	Milchshake	молóчный коктéйль	sữã sốc

Vocabulary Supplement   additional food, methods of cooking

Teaching Suggestions

1. Point to the item and model the sentence for the students.
   I am eating pizza. (french fries, etc.)
   I am drinking beer. (wine, a soft drink)
   Change the subject.
   You (He) are (is) eating pizza. (chips, etc.)
   You (He) are (is) drinking beer. (chips, etc.)
   Change the tense.
   I was (will be) eating pizza. (chips, etc.)
   I was (will be) drinking beer. (chips, etc.)
2. Point to a picture and ask the following questions. Direct the students to answer in complete sentences.
   What are you (we, etc.) eating/drinking?
   Were you eating pizza? (chips, etc.)
3. Complete the following with a logical answer.
   _____ is a pie with a crust, tomato sauce, cheese, and other toppings. (pizza)
   _____ are thinly sliced, deep-fried potatoes. (potato chips)
   _____ are narrow, length-wise cut potatoes which are deep-fried. (french fries)
   A kernel which bursts when heated is _____. (popcorn)

A _____ is a sweet snack. (candy bar)
A _____ should never be swallowed. (chewing gum)
A _____ is a piece of candy attached to a stick. (lollipop)
_____ is made from tomatoes and spices and is put on top of food to add flavor. (catsup)
_____ is yellow and many people like it on top of hot dogs. (mustard)
A _____ is a small, round piece of bread. (roll)
A _____ is a small, ring-shaped cake which is deep-fried. (doughnut)
A _____ is a small, cup-shaped cake. (cupcake)
A _____ is an alcoholic beverage which is carbonated. (beer)
_____ is an alcoholic beverage made from fermented grapes. (wine)
A _____ is a carbonated beverage which is nonalcoholic. (soft drink)
A _____ is a beverage made from milk and ice cream. (milk shake)

Activities

1. Which is your favorite food? Why?
2. On which food do you put catsup? Mustard?
3. Which of these foods do you eat at a movie?
4. Play Bingo. Read the completion statements from Teaching Suggestions number 3 as clues: the players cover up or draw an X through the answers. To determine one winner, ask the players to spell the word, give a definition, or to use them in a sentence.
5. Play "What am I?"
6. On the chalkboard scramble the letters of the vocabulary items. Have the students unscramble them and write the correct words on the line provided.
7. From this list, what would you eat for breakfast? Lunch? Dinner? A snack? Dessert?
8. Which of these foods are served hot? Cold?
9. Ask the students to choose one food or drink and give the recipe for it.
10. Discuss the four food groups. Do any of these vocabulary items belong to these groups?
11. You are a slice of potato about to be dropped into the hot oil. What would you say to the cook to prevent this?
12. If there were only one food or drink available throughout the world, which would you want it to be?
13. Where can you purchase a pizza? Gum? Popcorn? Continue with all the foods and drinks. How are they packaged?
14. Have the students find the prices for the items pictured in a newspaper or in a store. See who can "buy" all of them the cheapest. You will have to qualify their shopping list for them — a small pizza, a six ounce bag of chips, etc.

16. Parts of the Body

Vocabulary

English	Spanish	French	Italian	German	Russian	Vietnamese
forehead	frente	front	fronte	Stirn	лоб	trán
eyebrow	ceja	sourcil	sopracciglia	Augenbraue	бровь	lông mày
eyelash	pestaña	cil	ciglia	Wimper	ресница	lông mi
cheek	mejilla	joue	guancia	Wange	щека	má
tongue	lengua	langue	lingua	Zunge	язык	lưỡi
lip(s)	labio(s)	lèvre(s)	labbra	Lippe(n)	губа, губы	môi
tooth, teeth	diente, dientes	dent, dents	dente, denti	Zahn, Zähne	зуб, зубы	răng, các răng
lung	pulmón	poumon	polmoni	Lunge	лёгкие	phổi
rib	costilla	côte	costola	Rippe	ребро	xương sườn
stomach	estómago	estomac, ventre	stomaco	Bauch, Magen	желудок	bao tử
fingernail	uña (de la mano)	ongle (de main)	unghia	Fingernagel	ноготь пальца руки	móng tay
toenail	uña (del pie)	ongle (de pied)	unghia del piede	Fussnagel	ноготь пальца ноги	móng chân
hip	cadera	hanche	fianco	Hüfte	поясница	hông
thigh	muslo	cuisse	coscia	Oberschenkel	бедро	đùi
skin	piel	peau	pelle	Haut	кожа	da
muscle	músculo	muscle	muscolo	Muskel	мускул	bắp thịt

Vocabulary Supplement additional parts of the body

Teaching Suggestions

1. Point to the item and model the sentence for the students. Have them use the sentence to identify the pictures.
   This is my forehead. (eyebrow, eyelash, etc.)
   Change the possessive.
   This is your (her, his, our, their) forehead. (eyebrow, eyelash, etc.)
   Change the plural.
   These are your (her, his, our, their) foreheads. (eyebrows, eyelashes, etc.)
2. Point to a picture and ask the following questions. Direct the students to answer in complete sentences.
   What is this?   What are these?   Is this your forehead?   Is this his rib?   Is this her fingernail?   Are these our thighs?   Are these their tongues?   Are these your eyelashes?   Are these her toenails?   Are these their ribs?   Are these our lungs?
3. Complete the following with a logical answer.
   The _____ is between the eyebrows and the hairline. (forehead)
   The hair over the eyes is called an _____. (eyebrow)
   The hair on the eyelids is an _____. (eyelash)
   A _____ is below the eyes and between the nose and ears. (cheek)
   You can lick your lips with your _____. (tongue)
   The _____ are around the mouth. (lips)
   People bite and chew with _____. (teeth)
   A _____ is in the chest area and is used to supply oxygen to the body. (lung)
   The _____ are bones which extend from the spine toward the front of the body. (ribs)
   The _____ aids in digesting food. (stomach)
   A _____ grows at the tip of a finger. (fingernail)
   A _____ grows at the tip of a toe. (toenail)
   A _____ is a bone between the waist and thigh. (hip)
   A _____ is the part of the leg between the hip and the knee. (thigh)
   _____ covers the body. (skin)
   A _____ aids the body in moving. (muscle)

Activities

1. Change the completion statements from Teaching Suggestions number 3 to question form. Direct the students to write the answers on the line provided.
2. Play "What am I?"
   I am on the head.
   I am near the eyes.
   I am hair.
   What am I? (eyebrow)
3. On what part of the body is the forehead? The fingernail? Toenail? Thigh? The lips?
4. Draw a skeleton and label the body parts.
5. What are the five senses? Which of the senses can be associated with the lungs? The skin? Eyelashes? Tongue?
6. What does the stomach do? The lung? The ribs? Tongue? Eyelash? Muscle? With what system is it connected? (stomach-digestive)
7. Of these body parts, which do you think is unnecessary? Why?
8. What type of doctor would treat a problem with an eye? (ophthalmalogist, optometrist) Who would treat a skin disorder or problem? (dermatologist) (teeth — dentist; muscle, rib, thigh — orthopedic doctor; toenail — podiatrist; lung — thoracic or pulmonary doctor)
9. How many words can the students find in the word fingernail? (rain, lag, fat, nag, fig, etc.)

17. Laundromat and Parts of Clothing

Vocabulary

English	Spanish	French	Italian	German	Russian	Vietnamese
washing machine	lavadora	machine à laver	lavatrice	Waschmaschine	стиральная машина	máy giặt
dryer	secadora	séchoir	asciugatrice	Wäschetrockner	сушилка	máy sấy
detergent	detergente	lessive	detergente	Reinigungsmittel	стиральный порошок	bột giặt
laundry basket	cesta de ropa	panier à linge	cesta per la biancheria	Waschkorb	корзина для белья	rổ đựng đồ giặt
clothesline	cuerda de la ropa	corde à linge	corda per stendere il bucato	Wäscheleine	верёвка для белья	dây phơi
clothespin	pinza	pince à linge	molletta	Wäscheklammer	зажímка для белья	kẹp quần aó
iron	plancha	fer à repasser	ferro da stiro	Bügeleisen	утю́г	bàn ủi
ironing board	tabla de planchar	planche à repasser	asse da stiro	Bügelbrett	гладильная доскá	bàn để ủi quần aó
laundry tub	pila de lavar	bassine	lavandino	Waschwanne	стиральный бак	bồn xả đồ giặt
sleeve	manga	manche	manica	Ärmel	рукáв	tay aó
cuff	puño	manchette	polso	Manschette	манжéт	măng sét aó
button	botón	bouton	bottone	Knopf	пýговица	nút aó
zipper	cremallera	fermeture éclair	chiusura lampo	Reissverschluss	мóлния	dây khóa quần
pocket	bolsillo	poche	tasca	Tasche	кармáн	túi
collar	cuello (de la camisa)	col	colletto	Kragen	воротник	cổ aó
shoelace	cordón del zapato	lacet	lacci	Schuhband	шнурóк для óбуви	dây giãy

Vocabulary Supplement   clothing

Teaching Suggestions

1. Point to an item and model the sentence for the students. Have them use the sentence to identify the pictures.
   This is a washing machine. (dryer, etc.)
   Change the demonstrative.
   That is a washing machine. (dryer, etc.)
   Change to the plural.
   These (Those) are washing machines. (etc.)
2. Point to a picture and ask the following questions. Direct the students to answer in complete sentences.
   What is this/that?   What are these/those?   Is this a dryer?   Is that a zipper?   Are these clothespins?   Are those cuffs?
3. Complete the following with a logical answer.
   A _____ is a machine which cleans dirty clothes. (washing machine)
   A _____ is a machine which removes water from washed clothes. (dryer)
   _____ is a soap which is put into water to clean clothes. (detergent)
   A _____ is a big container used to carry dirty or clean clothes. (laundry basket)
   Clean wet clothes are hung on a _____ to dry. (clothesline)
   A _____ fastens laundry onto a clothesline. (clothespin)
   An _____ is an electrical appliance used to remove wrinkles from clothing. (iron)
   One irons clothing on an _____ . (ironing board)
   A _____ is a big deep sink in which clothes can be washed. (laundry tub)
   A _____ is the part of a garment which covers the arms. (sleeve)
   A _____ is a fold at the bottom of a sleeve or at the bottom of a slack leg. (cuff)
   A _____ is sewn onto a garment to fasten it. (button)
   A _____ has rows of teeth and fastens garments. (zipper)
   A _____ is a small piece of material sewn on clothing in which things can be placed. (pocket)
   A _____ is the part of a garment which encircles the neck. (collar)
   A _____ is used to tie shoes. (shoelace)

Activities

1. Do you have a washing machine? Dryer? Iron?
2. Who does your laundry? Where?
3. Have you ever ironed? Do you like to iron? What do you iron?
4. Play Bingo. Read the completion statements from Teaching Suggestions number 3 as clues; the players cover up or draw an X through the answers. To determine the one winner, ask the players to spell the words, use them in a sentence, or give a synonym or antonym.
5. What does a washing machine (dryer, detergent, etc.) do?
6. On the chalkboard scramble the letters of the vocabulary items. Direct the students to unscramble the letters and to write words on the line provided. (aaeiihhwsnnmgc — washing machine)
7. Give directions on how to do laundry to an alien from outer space. Try to include as many vocabulary items as possible.
8. Draw items of clothing or cut them out of newspapers, magazines, or a catalogue and label the parts.
9. You are a little boy's (girl's) jacket pocket. What are some of the things put into you?
10. Can you think of a garment or article of clothing that has all the items listed?
11. Where can you buy a washing machine? Dryer? Detergent? Clothesline? Iron? Button? Zipper? Shoelace?
12. Are you wearing anything which has a sleeve? Cuff? Button? Zipper? Pocket? Collar?
13. You have just invented the zipper. Tell us how you made it and how it can be used.

18. Dwelling

Vocabulary

English	Spanish	French	Italian	German	Russian	Vietnamese
entrance, lobby	entrada	entrée	entrata, ingresso	Vorhalle	вход, передняя	lối vào, phòng trước
mailbox	buzón	boîte aux lettres	casetta delle lettere	Briefkasten	почтовый ящик	hộp thư
elevator	ascensor	ascenseur	ascensore	Fahrstuhl	лифт	thang máy
fire escape	salida de emergencia	escalier de secours	uscita di sicurezza	Notausgang	пожарная лестница	lối thoát hỏa hoạn
doorbell	timbre	sonnette	campanello della porta	Klingel	дверной звонок	chuông cửa
doorknob	puño	poignée de porte	maniglia della porta	Türgriff	дверная ручка	nắm đấm cửa
keyhole	agujero de la llave	trou de la serrure	buco della serratura	Schlüsselloch	замочная скважина	lỗ khóa
chain lock	candado de cadena	chaîne	lucchetto	Kettenschloss	дверная цепóчка	khóa xích
radiator	radiador	radiateur	termosifone	Heizkörper	радиатор	máy sưởi bằng hơi nước
furnace	horno	chaudière	fornace	Ofen	обогреватель	lò sưởi
hot water heater	calentador de agua	chauffe-eau	riscaldatore ad acqua calda, scaldabagno	Boiler	паровóе отоплéние	máy làm nước nóng
smoke alarm	alarma de humo	avertisseur d'incendie	allarme antincendio	Rauchalarm	дымовáя сигнализáция	máy báo động khói lửa
thermostat	termostato	thermostat	termostato	Thermostat	термостáт	máy điều nhiệt
ceiling	techo	plafond	soffitto	Decke	потолóк	trần nhà
floor	suelo, piso	plancher	pavimento	Boden	пол	sàn nhà
balcony	balcón	balcon	balcone	Balkon	балкóн	lan can

Vocabulary Supplement   rooms

Teaching Suggestions

1. Point to an item and model the sentence for the students. Have them use the sentence to identify the pictures.

   I see an entrance. (mailbox, elevator, etc.) Change the subject.

   She (He, We, You, They) sees (see) an entrance. (mailbox, elevator, etc.) Change the tense.

   I will see (saw, have seen) an entrance.

2. Point to a picture and ask the following questions. Direct the students to answer in complete sentences.

   Do you see an entrance?   Does she see a mailbox?   Does he see an elevator? Do they see a fire escape?   Did you see a doorknob?   Did he see a keyhole? Did they see a radiator?   Will you see a furnace?   Will she see a smoke alarm? Will they see the balcony?

3. Complete the following with a logical answer.

   A person walks into a building through the _____. (entrance)

   Letters, bills, and magazines are delivered to a _____. (mailbox)

   An _____ is a machine which carries people and things up and down. (elevator)

   A _____ is an outside ladder used in an emergency. (fire escape)

   One presses a button to ring a _____. (doorbell)

   A _____ is a handle for opening and closing a door. (doorknob)

   One puts a key into a _____ to lock or unlock a door. (keyhole)

   A _____ is attached to the inside of a door to keep out intruders. (chain lock)

   A _____ is a heating device. (radiator)

   A _____ produces and circulates heat. (furnace)

   A _____ is a device that warms water. (hot water heater)

   A _____ sounds a buzzer or bell in case of fire. (smoke alarm)

   A _____ is a device used to regulate the temperature of a room or building. (thermostat)

   A _____ is the interior upper part of a room. (ceiling)

   A _____ is the interior part of a room where one stands. (floor)

   A _____ is a platform on the outside of a building. (balcony)

Activities

1. Where do you live? What is the address? Do you live in a house, apartment, condominium, duplex?

2. Have you ever lived in an apartment? Did or do you like it? Is there an advantage in living in an apartment rather than in a house?

3. Draw a floor plan of your home. Label the rooms and use all the vocabulary items you can.

4. Do you think smoke alarms should be required in all buildings?

5. Play Bingo. Read the completion statements from Teaching Suggestions number 3 as clues; the players cover up or draw an X through the answers. To determine one winner ask the player to use the words in a complete sentence.

6. Read the completion statements from Teaching Suggestions number 3 and direct the students to write the answer on the line provided. Mix up the order of the statements.

7. What is the purpose or function of a furnace? (hot water heater, doorbell, etc.)

8. Play "Add-ons."

   Teacher: I see an entrance.

   Student 1: I see an entrance with a mailbox.

   Student 2: I see an entrance with a mailbox and I see an elevator. Continue with all the vocabulary items.

9. Circle the items that have something to do with a door. Draw an X through the items that have something to do with heat.

10. What would you do if there was a fire in your home? Do you have an escape route? Draw an escape plan from your home.

11. Bring into the classroom some rental ads from a newspaper. Explain the abbreviations if necessary. Have the students write an ad for their own home.

12. Discuss a lease. Include one year, two year, rent with option to buy, utilities, fees, security deposit, cleaning deposit, etc.

13. You live in an apartment and you have very noisy neighbors. What do you do?

14. You have no hot water in your apartment. Whom do you contact to get it fixed?

15. You are a keyhole. Tell us about all the people you see walking through the apartment hallway.

19. Kitchen

Vocabulary

English	Spanish	French	Italian	German	Russian	Vietnamese
stove, oven	cocina, horno	fourneau, four	cucina a gas, forno	Herd, Ofen	плита́, духо́вка	lò, bếp lò
refrigerator, freezer	frigorífico, congelador	frigo, congélateur	frigorifero, reparto per surgelati	Kühlschrank, Gefrierfach	холоди́льник, морози́льник	tủ lạnh, máy làm đá lạnh
dishwasher	fregaplatos	machine à laver la vaisselle	lavastoviglie	Geschirrspül-maschine	посудомо́ечная маши́на	máy giặt
sink	pila, fregadero	évier	lavandino	Waschbecken	ра́ковина	bồn rửa chén
coffeemaker, pot	cafetera	percolateur, cafetière	caffettiera	Kaffeekanne	кофева́рка, кофе́йник	máy, bình pha cà phê
electric mixer	mezcladora eléctrica	mixeur	mescolatore elettrico	elektrisches Mischgerät	электроми́ксер	máy trộn bằng điện
saucepan	cacerola	casserole	pentola	Kochtopf	кастрю́ля	nồi
frying pan	sartén	poêle (à frire)	padella	Bratpfanne	сковоро́дка	chảo
teakettle	tetera	bouilloire, théière	bollitore	Teekessel	ча́йник	ấm đun chà
cabinet	gabinete	placard	armadietto	Schrank	шка́фчик для посу́ды	tủ
measuring cup	taza para medir	mesure	misurino	Messbecher	сосу́д для измере́ния	chén đo lường
can, bottle opener	abrelatas, abrebotellas	ouvre-boîte	apribottiglie	Dosenöffner, Flaschenöffner	открыва́лка	cái mở hộp, mở chai
egg beater	batidor (de huevos)	batteuse	frullino	Schneebesen	яйцере́зка	máy đánh trứng
carving (butcher) knife	cuchillo de trinchar	couteau à découper	trinciante, coltello da cucina	Vorlegemesser	нож для ре́зки мя́са	dao thái thịt (người bán thịt)
cutting, chopping board	tabla para cortar	planche à découper	tagliere	Hackbrett	доска́ для пригото́вления мя́са	thớt
baking pan	tartera	plat à four	teglia	Kuchenform, Backblech	фо́рма для пирога́	khuôn nướng

Vocabulary Supplement   food

Teaching Suggestions

1. Point to the item and model the sentence for the students.

   This is my stove. (refrigerator, etc.)

   Change the possessive/demonstrative.

2. Point to a picture and ask the questions.

   What is this/that?   What are these/those?   Is this your stove?   Are these your baking pans/frying pans?

3. Complete the following with a logical answer.

   I cook a meal on top of the _____. (stove)

   The _____ keeps my food cold. (refrigerator)

   A machine which cleans dirty dishes is a _____. (dishwasher)

   I can wash dishes in the _____. (sink)

   A _____ is an electric appliance for brewing coffee. (coffeemaker)

   An _____ is an appliance with two beaters for blending ingredients. (electric mixer)

   A _____ is a deep pot or kettle with a long handle. (saucepan)

   A _____ is a shallow kettle with a long handle. (frying pan)

   A _____ holds water and whistles when the water boils. (teakettle)

   A _____ is like a cupboard with a door and shelves or drawers for storage. (cabinet)

   A _____ is a cup used to determine the correct quantity of an ingredient in a recipe. (measuring cup)

   A _____ is a device used to open tin cans or glass jars. (can opener)

   An _____ mixes eggs. (egg beater)

   A _____ is a cutting instrument with a long, sharp blade. (butcher knife)

   A _____ is a small piece of wood on which food is cut. (cutting board)

   A _____ is a pan used for cooking cakes, breads, or pies. (baking pan)

Activities

1. Does your kitchen have a refrigerator? What kind is it? (one door, two door, three door, frostless, etc.) What color is it?

2. Do you have a stove? Oven? What kind is it? (Gas, electric, self-cleaning, convection, microwave, etc.)

3. What kinds of things does a measuring cup measure? (liquids, dry ingredients, 1/3, 1/4, 1/2, etc.)

4. Do you have a dishwasher in your kitchen or are you it?

5. What do you store in your kitchen cabinets?

6. Do you have an electric mixer? What do you use it for?

7. Play "What am I?"

8. Change the completion statements from Teaching Suggestions number 3 to questions and direct the students to write the answer on the line provided.

9. Circle the items which run on electricity. Draw an X through the items that you could wash in the kitchen sink.

10. What can be cooked in an oven? Saucepan? Frying pan? Baking pan?

11. Where could you buy a stove? Refrigerator? Dishwasher? Measuring cup? Cutting board? Saucepan?

12. Draw a kitchen and label all the vocabulary items.

13. You are a stove. Tell the class all the foods which are cooked on you in a day.

14. Give the class directions for making your favorite dish or meal. Include preparation, cooking, and cleanup.

15. Discuss the different types of cooking (boiled, fried, deep-fried, baked, broiled). What could you boil? In what? For how long?

20. Bathroom

Vocabulary

English	Spanish	French	Italian	German	Russian	Vietnamese
light switch	interruptor	interrupteur	interruttore	Lichtschalter	выключатель (электрическая)	nút bật đèn
light bulb	bombilla	ampoule	lampadina	Birne	лампочка	bóng đèn
medicine cabinet	gabinete de medicina	armoire de pharmacie	armadietto per medicine	Arzneischrank	аптéчка	tủ thuốc
mirror	espejo	miroir	specchio	Spiegel	зéркало	gương
scale	báscula	balance	bilancia	Waage	весы́	cân
soap dish	platito para el jabón	porte-savon	piattino da saponetto	Seifennapf	мы́льница	đĩa đựng xà bông
bath mat	alfombrilla del baño	tapis de bains	tappetino da bagno	Vorleger	ко́врик для вáнной	miếng trải phòng tắm
washcloth	toalla pequeña	gant de toilette	asciugamano piccolo	Waschlappen	бáнное полотéнце	khăn tắm
toilet	retrete, sanitario	toilettes, w.-c.	toletta, gabinetto	Toilette	туалéт	cầu tiêu, bàn phấn
toilet paper	papel higiénico	papier hygiénique	carta igienica	Klopapier	туалéтная бумáга	giấy vệ sinh
bathtub	bañera	baignoire	vasca da bagno	Badewanne	вáнна	bồn tắm
shower	ducha	douche	doccia	Dusche	душ	vòi sen
shower curtain	cortina de la ducha	rideau de douche	tende per la doccia	Duschvorhang	занавéска для вáнной	màn phòng tắm
towel rack	estante para las toallas	porte-serviettes	porta asciugamani	Handtuchhalter	вéшалка для полотéнец	giá mặc khăn
faucet	grifo	robinet	rubinetto	Hahn	кран	vòi nước
sink plug, stopper	tapón	bouchon	tappo per lavandino	Stöpsel	пробка для ráковины	nút đút

Vocabulary Supplement colors

Teaching Suggestions

1. Point to the item and model the sentence for the students. Have them use the sentence to identify the pictures.
   This is a light switch. (light bulb, etc.)
   Change to the definite article.
   This is the light switch. (light bulb, etc.)
   Change to the plural.
   These are some (the) light switches: (light bulbs, medicine cabinets, etc.)

2. Point to a picture and ask the following questions. Direct the students to answer in complete sentences.
   What is this?   Is this a mirror?   Is this the scale?   Is this a washcloth?   Is this the bathtub?   Are these the faucets?   Are these some light bulbs?   Are these the soap dishes?

3. Complete the following with a logical answer.
   One turns on a _____ upon entering a dark room. (light switch)
   A _____ provides light in a dark room. (light bulb)
   I put my aspirin and cold medicine in the _____ in the bathroom. (medicine cabinet)
   I look into a _____ to see my reflection. (mirror)
   I step onto a _____ to find out how much I weigh. (scale)
   I put the soap into a _____. (soap dish)
   I put a _____ on the floor to catch splashed tub water. (bath mat)
   I wash myself with a _____. (washcloth)
   A _____ has a bowl and a tank of water. (toilet)
   _____ is a narrow roll of paper. (toilet paper)
   I sit down and wash my body in a _____. (bathtub)
   I stand up and wash my body in the _____. (shower)
   I pull the _____ closed when I shower to keep the water in the tub. (shower curtain)
   A _____ is a bar attached to a wall on which towels are hung. (towel rack)
   Water comes out of a _____. (faucet)
   A _____ holds water in a sink or tub. (stopper)

Activities

1. Do you have a scale in your bathroom? Do you keep it in another room? If so, where? How much do you weigh? Do you want to gain or lose weight?

2. What is in your medicine cabinet?

3. Play Bingo. Read the completion statements from Teaching Suggestions number 3 as clues; the players cover up or draw an X through the answers. To determine one winner, ask the player to spell the words or to use them correctly in a sentence.

4. Play "What am I?"

5. Change the completion statements in Teaching Suggestions number 3 to questions; direct the students to write the answer on the line provided. (What do you wash yourself with?)

6. How many bathrooms do you have in your home? Is that enough? Does yours have anything else which is not pictured here?

7. Draw a bathroom and label the items.

8. Read a word and ask the students to give you another word associated with it. (light switch — electricity; faucet — water, etc.)

9. What color is your bathtub? Shower curtain? Faucet? Bath mat?

10. An alien from outer space is visiting you. Tell it what a bathtub is and how it is used.

11. Where do you buy a light switch? Light bulb? Faucet? Shower curtain? Washcloth? Towel rack?

12. Which vocabulary item pictured do you think is not needed? Why?

21. Household Items

Vocabulary

English	Spanish	French	Italian	German	Russian	Vietnamese
fireplace	chimenea	cheminée	caminetto	Kamin	камин	lò sưởi
stereo, record player, hi-fi	estéreo, el tocadiscos	chaîne haute fidélité	stereo, giradischi	Plattenspieler	стереопроигрыватель	máy âm thanh nổi, máy hát, hi fi
tape recorder	máquina de cinta magnetofónica	magnétophone	registratore	Tonbandgerät	магнитофон	máy thu băng
rocking chair	mecedora	berceuse, fauteuil à bascule	sedia a dondolo	Schaukelstuhl	кресло-качалка	ghế du
cushion	cojín	coussin	cuscino	Sitzkissen	диванная полушка	gối đệm
curtain rod	barra de cortinas	tringle à rideaux	bastone per tende	Gardinenstange	карниз для штóры	que treo màn
shade	persiana	abat-jour	persiane	Lampenschirm	штóра	màn che ánh sáng
radio	radio	radio	radio	Radio	радиоприёмник	máy thu thanh
closet	armario	placard	armadio a muro	Wandschrank	стенной шкаф	hộc đựng đồ
shelf	estante	étagère	palchetto, ripiano	Regal	полка	kệ
drawer	cajón	tiroir	cassetto	Schublade	ящик стола	ngăn kéo
bedspread	colcha, sobrecama	couvre-lit	copriletto	Bettdecke	покрывáло	tấm phủ giường
pillow case	funda de almohada	taie d'oreiller	federa del cuscino	Kissenbezug	наволочка	bao gối
mattress	colchón	matelas	materasso	Matratze	матрац	nệm
sheet	sábana	drap	lenzuolo	Betuch	простыня́	khăn giường
blanket	manta, cobija	couverture	coperta	Decke	одеяло	mền, chăn

Vocabulary Supplement   words related to stereos, radios, tape players

Teaching Suggestions

1. Point to the item and model the sentence for the students. Have them use the sentence to identify the pictures.
   This fireplace is mine. (stereo, tape recorder, etc.)
   Change the possessive pronoun.
   This fireplace is hers (his, yours, ours, theirs).
   Change to the plural.
   These fireplaces (stereos, tape recorders, etc.) are mine (his, hers, yours, ours, theirs).
2. Point to a picture and ask the following questions. Direct the students to answer in complete sentences.
   Is this fireplace mine?   Is this radio ours?
   Is this blanket theirs?   Is this drawer hers?   Is this closet yours?   Are these shades ours?   Are these shelves mine?   Are these cushions his?
3. Complete the following with a logical answer.
   I burn logs in a _____ to provide heat. (fireplace)
   I play records on a _____. (stereo)
   I play tapes or cassettes on a _____. (tape recorder)
   I sit and rock on a _____. (rocking chair)
   A _____ is a soft pad or pillow for a chair or couch. (cushion)

A _____ is a metal bar nailed to a wall over a window from which curtains are hung. (curtain rod)
A _____ is on a roller over a window which is raised and lowered. (shade)
Marconi invented the _____. (radio)
I hang my clothes in a _____. (closet)
A _____ in my closet holds my shoes. (shelf)
A _____ is a boxlike compartment in furniture which can be pulled out. (drawer)
A _____ is a decorative covering for a bed. (bedspread)
A _____ is a decorative and protective covering for a pillow. (pillow case)
A _____ supports a person who is sleeping on a bed. (mattress)
A _____ covers a mattress. (sheet)
A _____ keeps a person who is sleeping warm. (blanket)

Activities

1. Do you have a fireplace in your home? Where is it? Do you like it?
2. Do you have a closet in your bedroom? Is it big enough for your things? Is it neat?
3. Change the completion statements from Teaching Suggestions number 3 to question form and direct the students to write the answer on the line provided.
4. Circle the items which can be found in a living room. Draw an X through the items which can be found in a bedroom.
5. Draw a room in which all the vocabulary items are pictured.
6. Play "Add-ons."
   Teacher: I see a room with a fireplace.
   Student 1: I see a room with a fireplace and a stereo.
   Student 2: I see a room with a fireplace and a stereo next to a tape recorder.
   Continue with all the vocabulary items.
7. Discuss reel-to-reel recorder, cassette recorder, portable units, tracks, etc. Do you have a tape recorder or a cassette machine? What do you play on them? Can you record? If so, what do you record? How?
8. Discuss stereo, hi-fi equipment. 33-1/3, 45 and 78 RPM. Do you have a record player? Does it play the three speeds? What do you listen to? Where do you buy the records?
9. Where can you buy a curtain rod? Sheets? A tape recorder? Cushions?
10. What is the purpose or function of a shade? Shelf? Drawer? Fireplace?
11. In what room of a home would you be most likely to find these vocabulary items?
12. You are an old cushion. Convince your owner not to throw you out.
13. Choose one word and ask the students to make new words from its letters. (bedspread — bed, red, read, dead, etc.)

22. Personal Items

Vocabulary

English	Spanish	French	Italian	German	Russian	Vietnamese
razor, electric razor	máquina (eléctrica) de afeitar	rasoir (électrique)	rasoio (elettrico)	(elektrischer) Rasierapparat	бритва, электробритва	đồ cạo râu, cạo râu điện
shaving cream	crema de afeitar, jabón de afeitar	mousse à raser	crema da barba	Rasierschaum	крем для бритья	kem bôi cạo râu
deodorant	desodorante	déodorant	deodorante	Deodorant	дезодорáнт	thuốc khử mùi hôi
lipstick	lápiz de labios	rouge à lèvres	rossetto	Lippenstift	губнáя помáда	son môi
nail polish	esmalte	vernis pour ongles	smalto per unghie	Nagellack	лак для ногтéй	thuốc đánh móng tay
nail file	lima	lime à ongles	lima da unghie	Nagelfeile	пилка для ногтéй	duã móng tay
nail clippers	tijeras (de uñas)	coupe-ongles	fobicine da unghie	Nagelzange	щипцы для ногтéй	đồ cắt móng tay
tweezers	pinzas	pince à épiler	pinzetta	Pinzette	пинцéт	nhíp nhổ râu
toothbrush	cepillo de dientes	brosse à dents	spazzolino da denti	Zahnbürste	зубнáя щётка	bàn chải đánh răng
toothpaste	pasta dentífrica	dentifrice	dentifricio	Zahnpasta	зубнáя пáста	kem đánh răng
shampoo	champú	shampooing	shampoo	Haarwaschmittel	шампýнь	thuốc gội đầu
soap	jabón	savon	sapone	Seife	мыло	sà bông
hairdryer, blowdryer	secadora de pelo	sèche-cheveux	asciugacapelli	Fön	фен	máy sấy, thổi tóc
curlers, rollers	rulos	bigoudis	bigodini, ferro per arricciare i capelli	Lockenwickler	бигуди	ống uốn, cuốn tóc
hairbrush	cepillo	brosse à cheveux	spazzola per capelli	Haarbürste	щётка для волос	bàn chải chải tóc
comb	peine	peigne	pettine	Kamm	расчёска	lược

Vocabulary Supplement   parts of the body

Teaching Suggestions

1. Point to the item and model the sentence for the students. Have them use the sentence to identify the pictures.

    I am going to buy a razor. (shaving cream, deodorant, etc.)

    Change the subject.

    You (He, She, We, They) are (is) going to buy a razor. (shaving cream, deodorant, etc.)

    Change the tense.

    I was (will be) going to buy a razor. (shaving cream, deodorant, etc.)

2. Point to a picture and ask the following questions. Direct the students to answer in complete sentences.

    What are you going to buy?   What is he going to buy?   What are we going to buy?   What are they going to buy?   What will you be buying?   What will she be buying?   What will I be buying?   What were you going to buy?   What were they going to buy?   What was she going to buy?

3. Complete the following with a logical answer.

    A man shaves his beard with a _____.
    (razor)

    A man lathers his face with _____ before shaving. (shaving cream)

    People use _____ to eliminate body odor and perspiration. (deodorant)

    Females use _____ to put color on their lips. (lipstick)

    Females use _____ to put color on their nails. (nail polish)

    I file my nails with a _____. (nail file)

    I cut my nails with a _____. (nail clippers)

    I remove a sliver from my finger with _____. (tweezers)

    I brush my teeth with a _____. (toothbrush)

    I put _____ on my toothbrush to clean my teeth. (toothpaste)

    I wash my hair with _____. (shampoo)

    I wash my body with _____. (soap)

    I dry my wet hair with a _____. (hairdryer)

    Females put _____ into their hair to make it curly. (curlers)

    I brush my hair with a _____. (hairbrush)

    I comb my hair with a _____. (comb)

Activities

9. Circle the items you use on your head. Draw an X through the items you use on your hands. What is left? (deodorant)

10. Where can you buy a razor? Nail polish? Hairdryer? Continue with all the items.

11. Which items of those pictured don't you have? Why?

12. You are a hair stylist at a department store beauty salon. Give a demonstration of the latest tips or tricks for nail and hair care. Try to use as many of the vocabulary items as possible in your demonstration.

13. You have just invented soap. Convince us it is a useful item.

14. Your houseguest is a native of a recently discovered island. He/She was living in the Stone Age and is unfamiliar with all the vocabulary items. Explain to him/her what each one is and how it is used.

1. Play Bingo. Read the completion statements from Teaching Suggestions number 3 as clues; the players cover up or draw an X through the answers. To determine one winner, ask the player to tell on which part of the body the items are used. Play "What am I?"

2. On the chalkboard scramble the letters of the vocabulary items. Direct the students to unscramble the letters and write the correct word on the line provided. (ktplscii — lipstick)

4. What do you do with a razor? (shaving cream, deodorant, etc.)

5. Do you use lipstick? (nail polish, shaving cream, etc.)

6. On what part of the body do you use nail polish? (deodorant, tweezers, etc.)

7. Draw a body and label which items you would use on each body part.

8. Tell a young boy how to shave. Tell a young girl how to care for her nails. Tell a young girl how to shampoo her hair and how to set it.

23. Telephone and Television

Vocabulary

English	Spanish	French	Italian	German	Russian	Vietnamese
receiver	auricular	récepteur	ricevitore	Hörer	телефóнная трýбка	ống nghe
dial	marcar	cadran	quadrante	Wählerscheibe	дисковый набóрный щитóк	quay điện thoại
push buttons	botones automáticos	presse-boutons	telefono a tasti	Tasten	кнóпочный набóрный щитóк	nhấn nút
cord	cordón	fil	cordone	Schnur	шнур	dây
pay telephone booth	cabina del teléfono público	cabine téléphonique	cabina telefonica pubblica	Telefonzelle	телефóн-автомáт	trạm điện thoại công cộng
coin slots	aberturas para las monedas	fentes	fessura per gettoni	Münzeinwurfschlitze	отвéрстия для дéнег	ống bỏ tiền
coin return	devolver la moneda	fente de remboursement	recupero monete	Rückgabe	возврáт монéты	hộp đựng tiền trả lại
telephone book	guía telefónica	annuaire	elenco telefonico	Telefonbuch	телефóнная кнúга	điện thoại niên giám
television	televisor	télévision	televisione	Fernsehapparat	телевúдение	truyền hình, tivi
screen	pantalla	petit écran	schermo	Schirm	экрáн	màn ảnh
antenna	antena	antenne	antenna	Antenne	антéнна	dây trời, ăng ten
camera	cámara	appareil-photo	telecamera	Kamera	кáмера	máy ảnh
microphone	micrófono	microphone	microfono	Mikrofon	микрофóн	máy vi âm
news show	noticiario	informations	telegiornale	Nachrichtensendung	прогрáмма новостéй	mục tin tức
comedy show	comedia	revue comique	spettacolo comico	Unterhaltungssendung	эстрáдное представлéние	mục hài hước
commercial	anuncio	publicité, réclame	reclame, pubblicità	Reklame	реклáма	mục quảng cáo

Vocabulary Supplement phrases to place a telephone call, types of television programs

Teaching Suggestions

1. Point to the item and model the sentence for the students. Have them use the sentence to identify the pictures.
   I see a receiver. (dial, push buttons, etc.)
   Change the subject.
   You (She, etc.) see(s) a receiver.
   Change the tense.
   I saw (will see) a receiver. (dial, etc.)
2. Point to a picture and ask the following questions. Direct the students to answer in complete sentences.
   What do you see?   What does she see?
   What do we see?   What did you see?
   What will you see?   What will they see?
3. Complete the following with a logical answer.
   A _____ is a wheel with the numbers one through nine on it. (dial)
   A person talks into the _____ on a telephone. (receiver)
   I press the _____ to make a phone call. (push buttons)
   The telephone _____ contains wires and connects the telephone and receiver. (cord)
   When I am not at home I can make a telephone call from a _____. (telephone booth)
   I put money into the _____ to pay for a phone call. (coin slots)
   Money comes back to me in the _____ slot. (coin return)
   I look up telephone numbers in the _____. (telephone book)
   A _____ is a device on which one can see and hear programs. (television)
   I see the television picture on the _____. (screen)
   The _____ is a device which picks up the television transmission. (antenna)
   A television _____ takes the picture. (camera)
   A _____ picks up sound and amplifies or transmits it. (microphone)
   A _____ relates the day's events. (news show)
   A _____ is an entertaining, funny program. (comedy show)
   A _____ tries to sell a product to the television viewer. (commercial)

Activities

9. Write a television commercial for the product of your choice.
10. You are a newscaster. Give us today's news.
11. In your opinion, which is more useful, the telephone or television? Why?
12. In an emergency, do you need coins to place a telephone call from a booth?
13. What are some jobs or occupations related to the telephone and television? (telephone — operator, lineman, installer, repair person, etc.; television — camera operator, lighting technician, director, stage manager, writer, etc.) Discuss each.
14. If you can't speak or understand English (Spanish, French, etc.), can you request an operator who speaks a foreign language to assist you in making a phone call?
15. Is telephone service the same in France? Spain?
16. Are any American television programs shown in foreign countries? What do they do about the language?

1. Play "What am I?"
2. Divide the class into two groups and have a spelling bee. As elimination rounds are required, ask the players for the definite article, indefinite article, a demonstrative, etc.
3. Do you have a telephone? What is your telephone number? What is your area code? Can you dial long distance direct? Where is your telephone? What color is it? Is it a dial or push-button telephone? How often do you use it? Is your number listed?
4. Do you have a television? Where is it? Is it a color set or a black-and-white set? Is it a portable or a console? What size is the screen? What programs do you watch?
5. Draw a pay telephone and label all the parts.
6. Divide the class into groups of two. Direct them to make telephone calls to each other.
7. Make a telephone directory of the class.
8. Discuss other types of television programs (game shows, soap operas, cartoons, sports events, westerns, situation comedies, dramas, documentaries). Which is your favorite? Who is your favorite television actress and actor? Why?

24. Workshop

Vocabulary

English	Spanish	French	Italian	German	Russian	Vietnamese
workshop	taller	atelier	officina, bottega	Werkstatt	мастерскáя	xưởng
workbench	banco del taller	établi	banco di lavoro	Werkbank	рабóчий стол	ghế dài trong xưởng
toolbox	caja de herramientas	boîte à outils	cassetta da lavoro	Werkzeugkasten	инструментáльный ящик	hộp đồ nghề
wrench	llave inglesa	clef (à écrous)	chiave inglese	Schraubenschlüssel	гáечный ключ	kềm mỏ lết
screwdriver	destornillador	tournevis	giravite	Schraubenzieher	отвёртка	cái vặn vit
hammer	martillo	marteau	martello	Hammer	молотóк	búa đập
nail	clavo	clou	chiodo	Nagel	гвоздь	đinh
electric saw	sierra eléctrica	scie électrique	sega elettrica	elektrische Säge	электропилá	cưa điện
saw	sierra	scie	sega	Säge	пилá	cưa
pliers	alicates	pince	tenaglie	Zange	плоскогýбцы	kềm
tape measure	cinta para medir	mètre à ruban	metro a nastro	Bandmass	рулéтка	thước dây
drill	taladro	foret	trapano	Drillbohrer	дрель	khoan
ladder	escalera	échelle	scala	Leiter	лéстница	thang
paintbrush	brocha	pinceau	pennello	Anstrichpinsel	малярная кисть	chổi quét sơn
paint roller	arrollador de pintar	rouleau à peinture	rollo per pitturare	Walze	рóлик для покрáски	ống lăn sơn
flashlight	linterna	lampe de poche	lampadina tascabile	Taschenlampe	фонáрик	đèn bấm

Vocabulary Supplement   occupations related to tools

Teaching Suggestions

1. Point to the item and model the sentence for the students. Have them use the sentence to identify the pictures.

   This is my workshop. (toolbox, nail, etc.)
   Change the possessive adjective.
   This is his (your, etc.) workshop. (nails, etc.)
   Change the plural.
   These are my (his) workshops, (nails, etc.)

2. Point to a picture and ask the following questions. Direct the students to answer in complete sentences.

   What is this?   Is this your screwdriver?
   Is this their toolbox?   Are these his nails?

3. Complete the following with a logical answer.

   I work with tools and machines in a _____ .
   (workshop)
   In the workshop I work at a _____ .
   (workbench)
   I store my small tools in a _____ . (toolbox)
   A _____ is used to grip a nut or bolt. (wrench)
   A _____ is a tool used to turn screws.
   (screwdriver)
   A _____ pounds nails. (hammer)
   A _____ is pounded into two pieces of
   wood to fasten it. (nail)
   An _____ is a tool with a blade or disk
   which cuts wood. (electric saw)
   A _____ is a hand-held tool with a blade.
   (saw)

   A _____ is a tool with a pair of "jaws" used for holding or bending some object. (pliers)
   A _____ is used to determine the length, height, or width of an object. (tape measure)
   A _____ is a tool with a pointed end for boring holes into a hard material. (drill)
   A _____ is used to reach high places. (ladder)
   A _____ spreads paint on a wall. (paintbrush)
   A _____ is a long-handled roller used for painting. (paint roller)
   A _____ is a portable, battery-operated light. (flashlight)

Activities

1. Play "What am I?"
2. Change the completion statements in Teaching Suggestions number 3 to true-and-false statements. If the answer is false, ask the student for the correct answer.
3. On the chalkboard scramble the letters of the vocabulary items. Have a contest to see which student can unscramble them first. Direct the students to write the correct word on the line provided. (mmhrae — hammer) What do you do with a hammer? A pliers? A wrench? Continue with all the vocabulary items.
4. Do you know anyone who has a workshop? Who? What do they do in their workshop?
5. Which items would a plumber use? A carpenter? A painter?
6. What materials are the tools made of? (hammer — wooden handle, metal)
7. Who would use a toolbox in his/her job or occupation?
8. Have you ever used any of these tools? What for?
9. Are any of these tools dangerous? Why or how?
10. You are a ladder. Describe the people who use you and what they do.
11. You have just invented a new tool. What is it? What is it used for? Who would use it? When? How?
12. You are a nail about to be pounded into a piece of wood. What would you say to the hammer to try to stop this?

25. Gardening

Vocabulary

English	Spanish	French	Italian	German	Russian	Vietnamese
rake	rastro	râteau	rastrello	Harke	грабли	bồ cào
shovel	pala	pelle	pala	Schaufel	лопа́та	xẻng
hose	manguera	tuyau d'arrosage	tubo di gomma	Schlauch	шланг	ống dẫn nước
sprinkler	rociadera automática	arroseur	innafiatrice automatica	Rasensprenger	бры́згалка	cái tưới nước
sprinkling can	envase para rociar	arrosoir	innaffiatoio	Giesskanne	ле́йка	bình tưới nước
wheelbarrow	carretilla	brouette	carriola	Schubkarren	та́чка	xe cút kit
hoe	azada	sarcloir	zappa	Hacke	мотыга	cuốc
lawn, grass	césped, hierba	pelouse, le gazon	prato rasato, erba	Rasen	лужа́йка	luống cỏ, cỏ
lawnmower	cortadora de césped	tondeuse à gazon	falciatrice per prati	Rasenmähmaschine	коси́лка	máy cắt cỏ
grass catcher	recogehierba	ramasse-herbe	raccoglitore dell'erba	Grasfänger	траворе́зка	máy hót cỏ
clippers	tijeras	tondeuse	tosatrici, forbici per tosare	Schere	щипцы	kéo cắt cây
trowel	paleta	déplantoir	paletta da giardiniere	Ausheber	лопа́тка	cái bay
seed	semilla	semences	seme	Saat	се́мя	hạt
pot	tiesto	pot (de fleurs)	vaso	Topf	горшо́к для цвето́в	bình
houseplant	planta	plante	pianta da casa	Hauspflanze	дома́шнее расте́ние	cây cảnh
bush	arbusto	buisson	cespuglio	Busch	куст	bụi cây

Vocabulary Supplement   flowers and vegetables

Teaching Suggestions

1. Point to the item and model the sentence for the students. Have them use the sentence to identify the pictures.
    I have a rake. (shovel, hose, etc.)
    Change the subject.
    She (He, You, We, They) has (have) a rake. (shovel, hose, etc.)
    Change the tense.
    I (You, She, He, We, They) had (will have) a rake. (shovel, hose, etc.)

2. Point to a picture and ask the following questions. Direct the students to answer in complete sentences.
    What do you have?   What does she have?   What do we have?   What does he have?   What do they have?   Does she have a rake?   Does he have a rake?   Do we have a lawnmower?   Do they have a lawnmower?   Do we have a pot?   Did he have a trowel?   Did you have a wheelbarrow?   Did they have a hoe?   Will you have a houseplant?   Will we have a lawn?

3. Complete the following with a logical answer.
    I gather leaves with a ——— . (rake)
    I dig holes with a ——— . (shovel)
    A ——— carries water to the garden. (hose)
    A ——— spreads water on a lawn or garden. (sprinkler)

I water my plants with a ——— . (sprinkling can)
    A ——— is a push-type cart which has one or two wheels and is used to carry small loads. (wheelbarrow)
    A ——— has a long handle and a flat blade and is used for gardening. (hoe)
    ——— is green and covers the ground in front and back yards. (grass)
    A ——— is a machine which cuts grass. (lawnmower)
    A ——— is a bag attached to a lawnmower to hold the cut grass. (grass catcher)
    ——— are like a big pair of scissors and are used to trim bushes. (clippers)
    A ——— is a small, hand-held tool with a scoop-shaped blade. (trowel)
    A ——— is planted and from it a new plant sprouts or grows. (seed)
    A ——— is a container for a plant. (pot)
    A ——— is usually a small plant suitable for growing indoors. (houseplant)
    A ——— is a low plant with branches. (bush)

Activities

1. Play Bingo. Read the completion statements from Teaching Suggestions number 3 as clues; the players cover up or draw an X through the answers. To determine one winner, ask the player to spell the word or to give a definition.
2. Play "What am I?"
3. Change the completion statements from Teaching Suggestions number 3 to question form. Direct the students to write the answer on the line provided.
4. What is a rake (shovel, hose, etc.) used for?
5. Do you have any of these vocabulary items? Where do you keep them? What do you use them for?
6. Do you have any houseplants? What kind? How do you care for them?
7. Do you have a flower or vegetable garden? Where is it? What do you grow? How do you care for it? When do you plant the seeds?
8. You want the job of caring for a neighbor's lawn and garden. Convince the neighbor you will do the best job of all those applying. Try to use as many vocabulary items as you can in your sales presentation.
9. If you had a garden plot and could grow anything you wanted, what flowers and/or vegetables would you grow? Why?
10. Where could you buy a rake? (shovel, hose, etc.)
11. Do you think you or your family could save any money if you grew your own vegetables? What would you do over the winter?
12. You are a seed. Explain to the person who is going to plant you what you need to grow.

26. Sports Equipment

Vocabulary

English	Spanish	French	Italian	German	Russian	Vietnamese
soccer ball	balón	ballon	palla	Fussball	футбольный мяч	bóng tròn
football	fútbol americano	football américain	pallone	Fussball	мяч	túc cầu Mỹ
baseball mitt	manopla de béisbol	gant de base-ball	guanto da baseball	Baseballhand-schuh	бейсбольная перчатка	găng tay đá cầu
tennis racket and ball	raqueta y pelota de tenis	raquette, balle de tennis	racchetta da tennis e palla	Tennisschläger, Tennisball	тённисная ракётка и мячик	vợt và bóng ten nít
running shoes	zapatos de deporte	chaussures de sport	scarpe da corsa	Laufschuhe	спортивные туфли	giầy chạy
golf clubs, ball	palos y pelota de golf	crosse, balle de golf	circolo del golf, palla	Golfschläger, – ball	клюшки для гóльфа, мяч	gậy, banh đánh gôn
hockey stick, puck	palo y disco de hockey	crosse de hockey, palet	mazza da hockey, disco di gomma	Hockeyschläger, Eishockeyscheibe	клюшка, шайба	gậy, dĩa hockey
ice skates	patines (sobre hielo)	patins à glace	pattini da ghiaccio	Schlittschuhe	коньки	giầy trượt trên nước đá
roller skates	patines de ruedas	patins à roulettes	pattini a rotelle	Rollschuhe	ролики	giầy trượt bằng có bánh xe
basketball and hoop	baloncesto y aro	basket-ball, panier	pallacanestro, cesto	Basketball und Korb	баскетбóльный мяч и кольцó	bóng rổ và rổ
ping pong paddle, ball	raqueta y pelota de tenis de mesa	raquette, balle de ping pong	racchetta, palla da ping-pong	Tischtennisschläger, Tischtennisball	ракётка для пинг-понга и шарик	vợt, banh bóng bàn
bowling ball, pin	bola y clavijas	boule, quille	palla da bocce, birillo	Bowlingball, Kegel	кéгли	banh, chai chơi lăn banh
boxing gloves	manoplas de boxeo	gants de boxe	guanti da pugilato	Boxhandschuhe	боксёрские перчатки	găng đánh quyền anh
skis	esquís	skis	sci	Skier	лыжи	giầy trượt tuyết
fishing rod	caña_de pescar	canne à pêche	canna da pesca	die Angelrute	удочка	cần câu
hiking boots, backpack	botas de montaña, paquete	chaussures de marche, sac à dos	scarponi da montagna, zaino	Wanderstiefel, Rucksack	обувь для гóрного спóрта, рюкзáк	giầy đi bộ, túi deo lưng

Vocabulary Supplement places where sports are played

Teaching Suggestions

1. Point to the item and model the sentence.
   I have a baseball. (football, etc.)
   Change the subject; then change the tense.
2. Point to a picture and ask questions like these.
   What do you have?   What does she have?
3. Complete the following with a logical answer.
   A _____ is a round ball which the players kick or hit with their head. (soccer ball)
   A _____ is an oval-shaped ball. (football)
   A _____ is used to catch a baseball. (baseball mitt)
   Tennis is played with a _____ and _____. (racket, ball)
   _____ are shoes which are made of rubber and canvas. (running shoes)
   Golf is played with _____ and a _____. (clubs, ball)
   A hockey player hits the _____ with the _____. (puck, stick)

_____ are skates with blades. (ice skates)
_____ are skates with four small wheels. (roller skates)
In the game of basketball, one throws the _____ through a _____. (basketball, hoop)
In the game of ping pong, one hits the _____ with a wooden _____. (ping pong ball, paddle)
A _____ is a heavy ball with three holes in it, and it is rolled down an alley to knock down _____. (bowling ball, pins)
_____ are padded gloves worn by boxers. (boxing gloves)
_____ are attached to a boot and are used for gliding over the snow. (skis)
A _____ is used to catch fish. (fishing rod)
_____ are heavy boots. A _____ is like a knapsack on a frame. (hiking boots, backpack)

Activities

1. Play "What am I?"
2. On the chalkboard scramble the letters of the vocabulary items and direct the students to unscramble them and write the correct word on the line provided.
3. Do you have any of this sports equipment? Which? Where do you keep it (them)?
4. Do you like to watch sports activities? Where? Which sports?
5. Where is baseball played? Football? Tennis? Golf? Hockey? Bowling?
6. Which sports are played indoors? Outdoors? Which can be played in either place?
7. Which sports are played in the summer? In the winter? Either season?
8. Is any other equipment or special clothing needed to play football? Baseball? Hockey? To box? To ski? To ice skate? To roller skate?
9. Choose a sport and explain the rules to the class.
10. Do you participate in any of these sports? Which? Why?
11. Are any of these sports dangerous? Under what conditions? Have you ever been hurt playing a sport?
12. You have just thought of a new sport. What is it called? How many players is it for? Where is it played?
13. Which are team sports? How many members are on the team?
14. Do you think the life of a professional sports-person is an easy or glamorous life? Why or why not?

27. Infants

Vocabulary

English	Spanish	French	Italian	German	Russian	Vietnamese
baby, infant	bebé	bébé	bambino, neonato	Kind, Baby	мальш, ребёнок	trẻ sơ sinh
diaper	pañal	couche	pannolino	Windel	пелёнка	tã lót
crib	cuna	lit, berceau	lettino	Kinderbett	детская кроватка	nôi
baby bottle	biberón	biberon	biberon	Milchflasche	рожок	bình sữa bú
nipple	pezón	tétine	tettarella	Sauger	сóска	núm vú
baby food	comida de bebé	nourriture pour bébés	la pappa	Kinderspeise	пища для грудных детей	thức ăn con nít
carriage, buggy	cochecito	voiture d'enfant	carrozzino per bambini	Kinderwagen	детская коляска	xe con nít
stroller	silla	poussette	carrozzino scoperto	(Kinder)Sportwagen	лéтняя коляска	xe đẩy
car seat	asiento infantil para el coche	siège de voiture pour enfant	sedia da sicurezza per bambini	Kindersitz	сиденье в коляске	ghế em bé ngồi đi xe
rattle	sonajero	hochet	sonaglino	Kinderklapper	погремýшка	đồ chơi phát âm
high chair	trono	chaise haute	seggiolone	Kinderstuhl	высóкий стул	ghế em bé ngồi ăn
cradle	cuna	berceau	culla	Wiege	колыбéль	nôi
playpen	parque infantil	parc (pour enfants)	recinto per bambini	Laufgitter	дéтский манéж	cũi con nít
bib	babero	bavette	bavaglino	Lätzchen	дéтский нагрýдник	yếm, xây con nít
teething ring, pacifier	chupete	sucette, tétine	succhiotto	Zahnring, Schnuller	выпрямйтель для зубóв	vành để gặm của con nít mọc răng
safety pin	alfiler de seguridad	épingle de sûreté	spilla	Sicherheitsnadel	булáвка	kim găm

Vocabulary Supplement   care of a baby

Teaching Suggestions

1. Point to the item and model the sentence for the students. Have them use the sentence to identify the pictures.

   That is a baby. (diaper, crib, etc.)

   Change to the plural.

   Those are babies. (diapers, cribs, etc.)

   Add an appropriate adjective.

   This is a small baby. (white diaper, small crib, etc.)

2. Point to a picture and ask the following questions. Direct the students to answer in complete sentences.

   What is that?   What are these?   Is that a cradle?   Are those safety pins?   Is the baby food warm?   Is the high chair green?   Are the rattles yellow?   Is the playpen big?   Is the bib clean?

3. Complete the following with a logical answer.

   A recently born person is a _____ . (baby)

   A _____ is a folded cloth or other material put on a baby's bottom. (diaper)

   A baby bed with high sides is a _____ . (crib)

   A baby drinks from a _____ . (baby bottle)

   A _____ is a rubber cap on top of a baby bottle. (nipple)

Ground or strained food in small jars is _____ . (baby food)

A _____ has four wheels and a basket with a handle. (carriage)

A baby can sit in a _____ and be pushed around. (stroller)

A _____ is a device which secures a baby in an automobile. (car seat)

A _____ is a baby toy which makes noise when shaken. (rattle)

A baby sits in a _____ to be fed. (high chair)

A _____ is a baby bed which rocks. (cradle)

A _____ is a portable enclosure in which a baby can play. (playpen)

A _____ is put around a baby's neck to catch food. (bib)

A _____ massages a baby's gums when teeth are coming in. (teething ring)

A _____ is used to secure cloth diapers. (safety pin)

Activities

1. Play Bingo. Read the completion statements from Teaching Suggestions number 3 as clues; the players cover up or draw an X through the answer. To determine one winner, ask the player to give a definition of the word or to use it in a sentence.

2. Change the completion statements from Teaching Suggestions number 3 to question form. Direct the students to write the answer on the line provided.

3. Do you like babies? Why or why not?

4. What do babies do? (cry, eat, sleep, play, etc.)

5. What is a crib (carriage, high chair, etc.) used for?

6. Where can you buy diapers? Baby food? A high chair? Continue with all the vocabulary items.

7. Have you ever cared for a baby? Whose baby was it? What did you do?

8. Try to explain to a baby the proper way to eat.

9. You are walking a baby in a stroller. Explain to the baby the following: the sky, birds, cars, horns honking, trees, flowers.

10. Do you think babies should be born knowing how to talk?

11. Describe a typical day in the life of a baby. Try to use all the vocabulary items.

12. You have just invented the safety pin. Convince a mother it is useful and will not hurt her baby.

13. Do you think car seats for babies should be required by law?

28. Leisure Activities

Vocabulary

English	Spanish	French	Italian	German	Russian	Vietnamese
dance	baile	danse	danza, ballo	Tanz	тáнец	khiêu vũ
concert	concierto	concert	concerto	Konzert	концéрт	hòa nhạc
movie	película	film	film	Film	кинó	chiếu bóng
sporting event	espectáculo deportivo	épreuves sportives	evento sportivo	Sport	спортúвное состязáние	trận đấu thể thao
theater	teatro	théâtre	teatro	Theater	теáтр	rạp hát
television	televisión	télévision	televisione	Fernsehen	телевúдение	truyền hình, tivi
video game	juego electrónico	jeu vidéo	gioco televisivo	Videospiel	телеигрá	trò chơi truyền hình
party	fiesta	soirée	festa	Party	приятельская встрéча	cuộc họp mặt
carnival, fair	carnaval	carnaval, foire	carnevale, fiera	Jahrmarkt	карнавáл, ярмарка	hội chợ
picnic	picnic, excursión al campo	pique-nique	scampagnata, picnic	Picknick	пикнúк	picnic, cuộc ăn chơi ngòai trời
cards	cartas	cartes	carte da gioco	Karten	кáрты	bài tây(bridge,xì phé)
chess	ajedrez	jeu d'échecs	scacchi	Schach	шáхматы	trò đánh cờ
checkers	damas	jeu de dames	dama	Dame	шáшки	cờ dam
crossword, jigsaw puzzle	crucigrama, rompecabezas	mots croisés, puzzle	parole crociate, rompicapo	Kreuzworträtsel, Zusammensetzspiel	кроссвóрд, головолóмка	ô chữ
toys	juguetes	jouets	giocattoli	Spielzeug	игрýшки	đồ chơi
exercise	ejercicios	exercice	esercizio	Gymnastik, Bewegung	упражнéние	thể dục

Vocabulary Supplement   related activities

Teaching Suggestions

1. Point to the item and model the sentence for the students. Have them use the sentence to identify the pictures.

   I am going to a dance. (concert, etc.)
   I am going to play cards. (chess, etc.)

   Change the subject.

   You (He) are (is) going to a dance. (party, etc.)
   You (He) are (is) going to play cards. (party, etc.)

   Change the tense.

   I was (will be) going to a dance. (party, etc.)
   I was (will be) playing cards.

2. Point to a picture and ask the following questions. Direct the students to answer in complete sentences.

   Where are you going?   Where is she going?   Where are they going?   What are you going to play?   What are we going to play?   What is she going to play?   Where will they be going?   Where will I be going?   Will he be playing chess?   Will they be playing checkers?

3. Complete the following with a logical answer. Two people move to the rhythm of music at a _____ . (dance)

People listen to a vocal group sing or an orchestra play at a _____ . (concert)
A _____ is a motion picture. (movie)
A tennis match is a _____ . (sporting event)
Actors perform a play in a _____ . (theater)
Some people relax by watching entertaining programs on _____ . (television)
A _____ is a game played on a television screen. (video game)
A _____ is a gathering of people to celebrate some event. (party)
A _____ is an outdoor amusement with rides and game booths. (carnival)
A _____ is a meal eaten outdoors. (picnic)
Bridge, hearts and war are games played with _____ . (cards)
_____ is a board game for two players with 16 chessmen. (chess)
_____ is a game played on a checkerboard by two persons, each with 12 checkers. (checkers)
A _____ is a puzzle in which the player reads clues to determine a word. (crossword puzzle)
An object for children to play with is a _____ . (toy)
Push-ups are types of _____ . (exercise)

Activities

1. Change the completion statements from Teaching Suggestions number 3 to question form. Direct the students to write the answer on the line provided.

2. Play "Add-ons."
   - Teacher: I am going to a dance.
   - Student 1: I am going to a dance and a concert.
   - Student 2: I am going to a dance and a concert, and tomorrow I am going to a movie.

   Continue with all the vocabulary items.

3. Do you play any card games? Which? What are the rules? How many players can play?

4. Do you know how to play chess? Checkers? Do you like to play?

5. Have you ever been on a picnic? Where did you have it? What did you eat?

6. What is your favorite movie? Who are the stars? What is the plot?

7. Where would you attend a dance? Concert? Play cards?

8. Draw a circle around the activities you can do alone. Draw an X through the activities for which you need another person.

9. Which of these activities can be enjoyed outdoors? Indoors? Either place?

10. Choose one activity in which you have participated and describe it to the class.

11. In your opinion, is exercising a relaxing activity?

12. You are planning a surprise party. Whom is it for? When? Where? For what occasion? Whom are you inviting? Are you going to decorate? Are you going to serve any food?

13. Do you enjoy some other activity during your leisure time? Which one?

14. Which of the pictured activities would you like to see eliminated? Why?

15. Have you ever played a video game? Where? Which one?

Vocabulary

English	Spanish	French	Italian	German	Russian	Vietnamese
happy	feliz	heureux, heureuse	felice	froh	счастливый	vui sướng
sad	triste	triste	triste	traurig	грустный	buồn
tired, sleepy	cansado, tener sueño	fatigué, -e	stanco, assonnato	müde, schläfrig	усталый, сонный	mệt, buồn ngủ
thirsty	tener sed	avoir soif	assetato	durstig	испытывать жажду	khát
hungry	tener hambre	avoir faim	affamato	hungrig	голодный	đói
cold	tener frío	avoir froid	freddo	kalt	хо́лодно	lạnh
hot, warm	tener calor	avoir chaud	bollente, caldo	heiss, warm	жа́рко	nóng, ấm
sick	enfermo	malade	ammalato	krank	больной	bình
well, fine	bien	bien, en bonne santé	bene	gesund	хорошо, прекрасно	khỏe, mạnh
hurt	dañado, lesionado	blessé, -e	male	gekränkt, verletzt	раненый	đau
afraid, frightened	tener miedo	avoir peur	paura, impaurito	bange	боящийся, испуганный	sợ, hãi
angry	enojado	fâché, -e, en colère	arrabbiato	ärgerlich, böse	злой	giận
surprised	sorprendido	étonné, -e	sorpreso	überrascht	удивлённый	ngạc nhiên
shy	tímido	timide	timido	scheu	застенчивый	mắc cỡ
worried	preocupado	inquiet, inquiète	preoccupato	beunruhigt	обеспокоенный	lo
bored	aburrido	ennuyé, -e	annoiato	gelangweilt	скучающий	chán

Vocabulary Supplement   noun forms of "feeling" adjectives

Teaching Suggestions

1. Point to the item and model the sentence for the students. Have them use the sentence to identify the pictures.

   I am happy. (sad, tired, etc.)

   Change the subject.

   He (You, She, We, They) is (are) happy. (sad, tired, etc.)

   Change the tense.

   I (You, She, He, We, They) was (were, will be) happy. (sad, tired, etc.)

2. Point to a picture and ask the following questions. Direct the students to answer in complete sentences.

Are you happy?	Is he sad?
Are they tired?	Is she thirsty?
Are they hungry?	Were you cold?
Was he warm?	Were we sick?
Were they well?	Will you be hurt?
Will he be afraid?	Will they be angry?
Will I be surprised?	Will we be worried?

3. Complete the following with a logical answer.

   When I smile I am _____. (happy)

   When I cry. (sad)

   I am _____ when I need sleep. (tired)

   I am _____ if I need something to drink. (thirsty)

   I am _____ when I want to eat something. (hungry)

   In the winter I feel _____. (cold)

   In the summer I feel _____. (hot)

   When my stomach is upset I feel _____. (sick)

   When nothing is wrong with me I feel _____. (well)

   If I fall down I feel _____. (hurt)

   I am _____ when I see a spider. (afraid)

   I am _____ in an argument. (angry)

   I am _____ there is a party for me. (surprised)

   I feel _____ when I meet a new person. (shy)

   I am _____ when I fail a test. (worried)

   I am _____ when I have nothing to do. (bored)

Activities

1. Change the completion statements from Teaching Suggestions number 3 to true and false. Direct the students to write the correct answer on the line provided if the answer is false.

2. Have the students take turns pantomiming the feelings. The other students can guess which feeling they are expressing.

3. Give antonyms for the feelings.

4. Give synonyms for the feelings.

5. What makes you happy? (sad, tired, thirsty, etc.)

6. You are a robot. Tell us the advantages and disadvantages of not having any feelings.

7. Describe your happiest day (your saddest day), either real or imaginary.

8. What do you do when you are sick? (tired, bored, hurt, afraid, etc.)

9. Make up a movie plot in which your star experiences all these feelings.

10. Which feeling would you eliminate? Why?

11. Is there a song or piece of music which makes you feel happy or sad?

12. What do you feel like when you are tired? Happy? Sad? Afraid? Worried? (tired — sluggish, droopy; try to elicit more adjectives)

30. Antonyms

Vocabulary

English	Spanish	French	Italian	German	Russian	Vietnamese
big	grande	grand, -e	grande	gross	большой	lớn
little	pequeño	petit, -e	piccolo	klein	маленький	nhỏ
tall	alto	grand, -e	alto	gross	высокий	cao
short	bajo	petit, -e	basso	klein	низкий	thấp
happy	feliz	heureux, heureuse	felice	glücklich	счастливый	vui
sad	triste	triste	triste	traurig	грустный	buồn
fast	rápido	rapide	veloce	schnell	быстрый	nhanh
slow	despacio	lent, -e	lento	langsam	медленный	chậm
wide	ancho	large	largo	breit	широкий	rộng
narrow	estrecho	étroit, -e	stretto	eng	узкий	hẹp
hot	caliente	chaude, -e	caldo	heiss	тёплый	nóng
cold	frío	froid, -e	freddo	kalt	холодный	lạnh
strong	fuerte	fort, -e	forte	stark	сильный	mạnh
weak	débil	faible	debole	schwach	слабый	yếu
up	arriba	en haut	sopra	nach oben	вверх	trên
down	abajo	en bas	sotto	nach unten	вниз	dưới

Vocabulary Supplement   objects depicting the antonyms

Teaching Suggestions

1. Point to the item and model the sentence for the students. Have them use the sentence to identify the pictures.

   The elephant is big.
   The boy is tall.
   The girl is happy.
   The rabbit is fast.
   The chair is wide.
   The soup is hot.
   The man is strong.
   The stairs go up.

   The mouse is little.
   The boy is short.
   The girl is sad.
   The turtle is slow.
   The chair is narrow.
   The ice is cold.
   The man is weak.
   The stairs go down.

2. Point to a picture and ask the following questions. Direct the students to answer in complete sentences.

   What is big?   Who is strong?   Where is the narrow road?   What is hot?   Where do the stairs go?   Who is sad?   Who is happy?   What is cold?   Who is short?

3. Complete the following with a logical answer.

   Huge is the same as ———. (big)
   Small is the same as ———. (little)
   Having great height is the same as being ———. (tall)
   Having little height is the same as being ———. (short)
   Having great pleasure is the same as being ———. (happy)
   Being unhappy is the same as being ———. (sad)

   Having great speed is the same as being ———. (fast)
   Having little speed is the same as being ———. (slow)
   Having great breadth is the same as being ———. (wide)
   Having a small width is the same as being ———. (narrow)
   Having great heat is the same as being ———. (hot)
   Having a low temperature is the same as being ———. (cold)
   Having great power is the same as being ———. (strong)
   Having little strength is the same as being ———. (weak)
   Going from a lower to a higher position is the same as going ———. (up)
   Going from a higher to a lower position is the same as going ———. (down)

Activities

1. Play Bingo. Read the completion statements from Teaching Suggestions number 3 as clues; the players cover up or draw an X through the answers. To determine one winner, ask the player to give a synonym or another antonym for the words.

2. Change the completion statements from Teaching Suggestions number 3 to question form. Direct the students to write the answer on the line provided.

3. Play "Add-ons."
   Teacher: I see a big elephant.
   Student 1: I see a big elephant and a small fly.
   Student 2: I see a big elephant and a small fly on a tall boy.

   Continue with all the vocabulary items.

4. What are some additional objects which could depict the eight pairs of antonyms?

5. Give synonyms for the antonyms. (fast — speedy; slow — sluggish, etc.)

6. Have a contest to see which student or group of students can list the most additional antonyms.

7. Have each student pick one pair of antonyms and tell why it is better to be one of them rather than the other. For example, it is better to be happy than sad because you will have more friends, you will live longer, etc. Have students do the same with the new list of antonyms which they made up in number 6 above.

31. Emergencies

Vocabulary

English	Spanish	French	Italian	German	Russian	Vietnamese
fire, burn	incendio, quemadura	incendie, feu	fuoco, bruciatura	Feuer, brennen	огóнь, ожóг	cháy, bỏng
car accident	accidente de automóvil	accident de voiture	incidente automobilistico	Autounfall	автомобильная авария	tai nạn xe hơi
pedestrian (hit-run) accident	accidente de peatón	piéton blessé par une voiture	investimento	Fahrerflucht	дорóжное происшéствие	tai nạn đụng người đi bộ (cán người-bỏ chạy)
bike accident	accidente de bicicleta	accident de bicyclette	incidente con la bicicletta	Radunfall	велосипéдная авария	tai nạn xe đạp
drowning	ahogo	noyade	annegato	Ertrinken	гибель на водé	sự chết đuối
robbery, mugging	robo	vol, agression	furto	Raub	грабёж, кража	cướp, đánh trộm
fall	caerse	chute	caduta	Sturz	падéние	ngã, té
choking	atragantamiento	étouffement	soffocazione	Ersticken	удýшье	ngộp thở
plane crash	estallido de avión	accident d'avion	incidente aereo	Flugzeugabsturz	áвиакатастрóфа, катастрóфа	tai nạn máy bay
tornado, hurricane	tornado, huracán	tornade, ouragan	ciclone, uragano	Wirbelsturm	урагáн	bão lốc, phong ba
explosion	explosión	explosion	esplosione	Knall	взрыв	nổ
heart attack	ataque de corazón	crise cardiaque	attacco cardiaco	Herzschlag	сердéчный прúступ	đứng tim (ngưng đập)
gun shot	disparo (de pistola)	coup de feu	colpo di arma da fuoco	Schuss	выстрел из пистолéта	bị bắn
cut	corte, lesión	blessure, coupure	taglio	Schnittwunde	порéз	bị đứt
flood	inundación	inondation	alluvione	Hochwasser	наводнéние	lụt
knocked out, unconscious	inconsciente	assommé, -e, inconscient, -e	privo di sensi, inconscio	bewusstlos, ohnmächtig	сбúтый с ног, потерявший сознáние	ngất

Vocabulary Supplement   related situations

Teaching Suggestions

1. Point to the item and model the sentence for the students. Have them use the sentence to identify the pictures.
   This is a fire. (car accident, etc.)
   Change the demonstrative; change to the plural.
2. Point to a picture and ask the following questions. Direct the students to answer in complete sentences.
   What is (are) this/that (these/those). Is this a plane crash? Is that a flood?
3. Complete the following with a logical answer.
   A burning house is on _____ . (fire)
   When two cars collide there is a _____ . (car accident)
   When a car hits a person walking there is a _____ . (pedestrian accident)
   When a person falls off a bicycle there is a _____ . (bicycle accident)
   When a person cannot breathe in water there is a _____ . (drowning)
   When one person steals something from another there is a _____ . (robbery)

   If a person drops from a ladder there is a _____ . (fall)
   When food or some other object is stuck in a person's throat that person is _____ . (choking)
   When an airplane collides with another plane or with the ground there is a _____ . (plane crash)
   A very strong wind which can destroy and move houses is a _____ . (tornado)
   A sudden, violent bursting of an object is an _____ . (explosion)
   A _____ is a failure of the pumping action of the heart. (heart attack)
   When a bullet is fired from a gun there is a _____ . (gunshot)
   A knife penetrating skin will produce a _____ . (cut)
   An overflowing or overabundance of water will produce a _____ . (flood)
   When a person receives a hard blow to the head and cannot be awakened, that person is said to be _____ . (knocked out)

Activities

1. Play Bingo. Read the completion statements from Teaching Suggestions number 3 as clues; the players cover up or draw an X through the answers. To determine one winner, ask the players to spell the words or to use them in a sentence.
2. Scramble the letters of the vocabulary items on the chalkboard. Have the students write the correct words on the line provided. (gnnrwdoi — drowning)
3. Do you know any first aid? Have you ever taken such a course? Where can you take a first aid course?
4. Have you ever been in a car accident? What happened? Where? When? Was anyone hurt? Did the police come? Was an insurance claim filed?
5. What would you do if you saw a pedestrian accident? A bicycle accident? A drowning? Someone who has fallen from a ladder?
6. Divide the class into groups of two. Assign each group an emergency. Direct the groups to prepare a phone call to the proper authorities to report the emergency.
7. Describe the feeling you think a person would have whose home is on fire, a person sighting a tornado, a person falling from a ladder, and a person cutting a finger on a knife.
8. Besides a flood and hurricane, what are some other natural disasters? (earthquake, drought, avalanche, etc.)
9. Do you know anyone who has been a victim of one of these emergencies? Which one? What happened?
10. How do you think you would react in an emergency?

Vocabulary

English	Spanish	French	Italian	German	Russian	Vietnamese
needle	aguja	aiguille	ago	Nadel	иголка	kim đan
thread	hilo	fil	filo	Faden	нитка	chỉ
straight pins	alfileres	épingles	spillo	Stecknadel	булавки	kim may thẳng
thimble	dedal	dé à coudre	ditale	Fingerhut	напёрсток	đê khau
sewing machine	máquina de coser	machine à coudre	macchina da cucire	Nähmaschine	швейная машина	máy may
pattern	patrón	patron	modello	Muster	выкройка	mẫu
material, fabric	tela	tissu	stoffa	Stoff	материáл, ткань	vải
seam	costura	couture	cucitura	Naht	шов	đường may
pin cushion	alfiletero	pelote à épingles	cuscinetto per spilli	Nadelkissen	подушечка для иголок	đệm cắm kim
scissors, shears	tijeras	ciseaux	forbici	Schere	ножницы	kéo, kéo lớn
knitting needles	agujas de malla	aiguille à tricoter	ferri di calza	Stricknadeln	вязáльные спицы	kim đan
crochet hook	gancho de crochete	crochet	uncinetto	Häkelnadel	вязáльный крючок	kim móc
yarn	lana (hilo)	laine	filato	Garn	пряжа	chỉ sợi
embroidery hoop	bastidor para bordar	tambour (de broderie)	telaio	Stickrahmen	пяльцы с зажимом	vòng để thêu
latch hook	gancho de aldabilla	crochet	gancio	Zungennadel		cái móc cài
rug canvas	lona de alfombra	canevas de tapis	canovaccio per tappeti	Kanevas	холст	vải bỏ làm thảm

Vocabulary Supplement   additional sewing terms and crafts

Teaching Suggestions

1. Point to the item and model the sentence for the students. Have them use the sentence to identify the pictures.

   I have a needle. (thread, straight pins, etc.)

   Change the subject.

   She (He, You, We, They) has (have) a needle. (thread, straight pins, etc.)

   Change the tense.

   I (She, He, You, We, They) had (will have) a needle. (thread, straight pins, etc.)

2. Point to a picture and ask the following questions. Direct the students to answer in complete sentences.

   What do you have?   What does she have?
   What will he have?   Did you have a pattern?   Will they have a sewing machine?   Did we have a thimble?

3. Complete the following with a logical answer.

   A small, thin sewing device with a sharp point on one end and an eye on the other end is a _____ . (needle)

   I put _____ through the eye of the needle. (thread)

   A short, straight piece of wire with a sharp point and a blunt end is a _____ . (straight pin)

   I put a _____ on my finger to protect it while I am sewing. (thimble)

   A _____ is a machine which makes stitches. (sewing machine)

   A _____ is a piece of paper imprinted with the parts of a garment. (pattern)

   _____ is cloth from which something is sewn. (material)

   A _____ is a line formed by sewing together two pieces of material.(seam)

   I put my straight pins in my _____ . (pin cushion)

   A pair of _____ is a tool for cutting fabric. (scissors)

   _____ are long thin instruments used in knitting. (knitting needles)

   A _____ is a tool used to crochet. (crochet hook)

   _____ is the material used in knitting and crocheting. (yarn)

   An _____ holds the material on which decorative stitches are made. (embroidery hoop)

   A _____ is a tool used in hooking rugs. (latch hook)

   A _____ is a loosely woven fabric used in hooking rugs. (rug canvas)

Activities

1. Change the completion statements from Teaching Suggestions number 3 to true-and-false statements. If the statement is false, ask the student to correct it by supplying the right answer.

2. Play "What am I?"

3. Change the completion statements in Teaching Suggestions number 3 to question form. Direct the students to write the answer on the line provided.

4. Have you ever taken a sewing course in school? Which department offers the course?

5. Where can you learn how to knit or crochet?

6. Do you know how to sew? To knit? To crochet? To hook a rug? To embroider? Who taught you? If so, what have you made?

7. Have you ever received a hand-made item as a gift? What was it? Who made it?

8. Is sewing a practical skill to know? Why?

9. Why do you think so many people, including men, enjoy handcrafts so much?

10. What other crafts are there that are not pictured here?

11. What is your hobby? Why did you choose it?

12. Would you pay more or less for a hand-crafted item?

13. Is there a craft which is done only in your area of the country? (seashore — shell jewelry) Are there any American crafts? French crafts? Spanish crafts? Italian crafts? Russian crafts? What are they? How or why do you think these became popular with the people? Was it because there was a need for the objects made?

Notes

Notes

1. School

Name_____

Date_____

Teacher_____

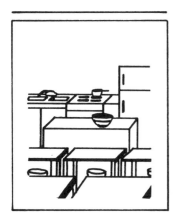 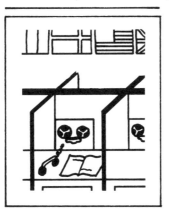  

 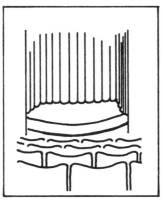  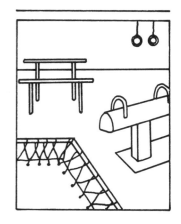

2. The Bank

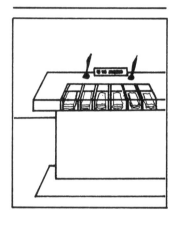
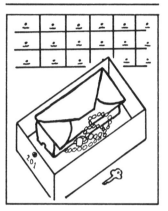
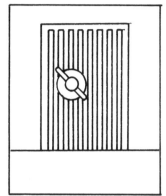
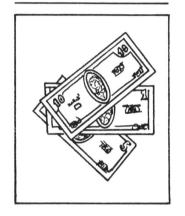

3. Doctor and Hospital

Name_____

Date_____

Teacher_____

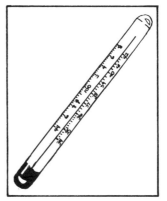
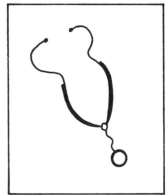

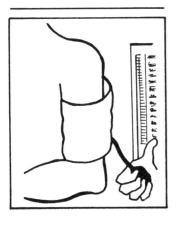
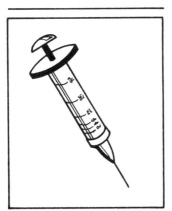

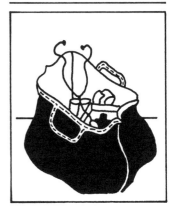

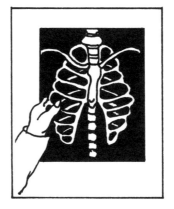
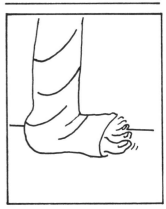

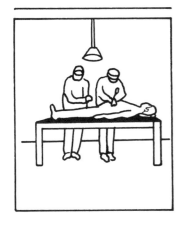

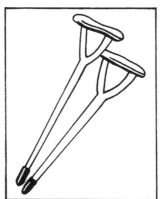

4. Post Office

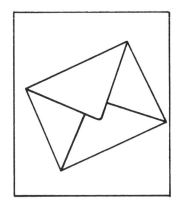

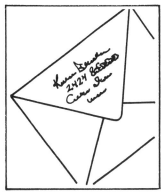

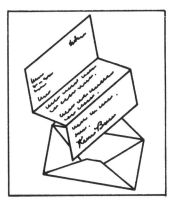

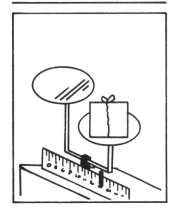
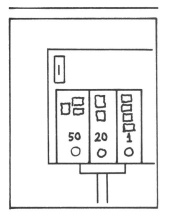

5. Police and Fire

Name_____

Date_____

Teacher_____

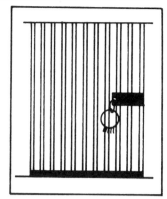

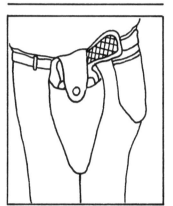

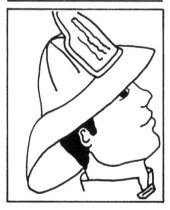

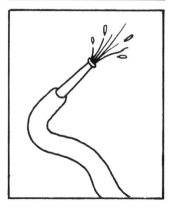
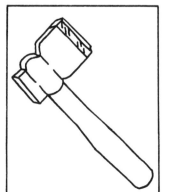

6. Mass Transportation

Name_____

Date_____

Teacher_____

   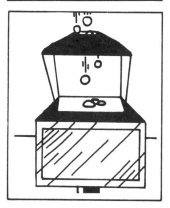

  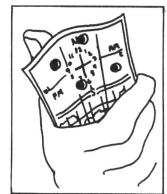 

7. Airport

 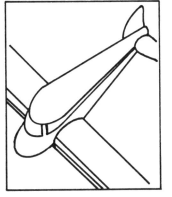  

 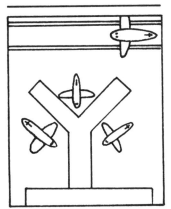 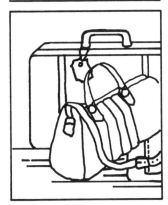 

 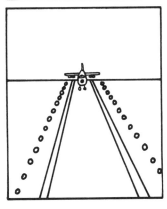 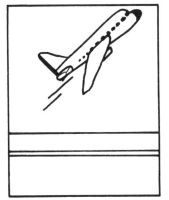

8. Car

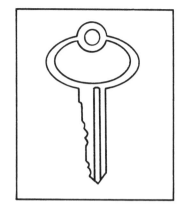
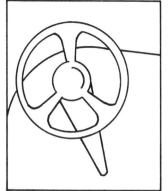
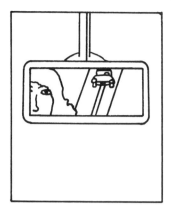
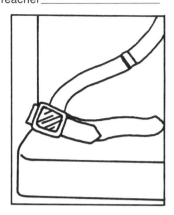

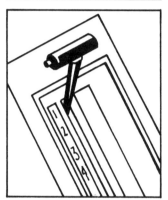
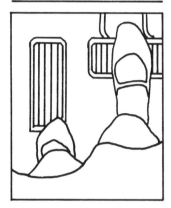

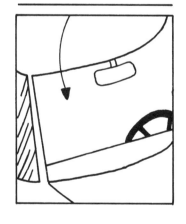

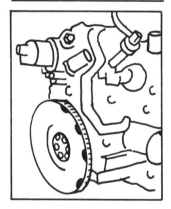
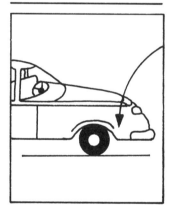

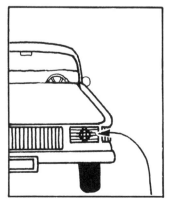
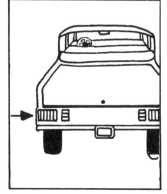

9. Road Signs

Name_____

Date_____

Teacher_____

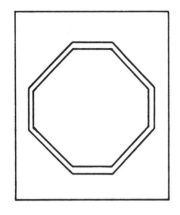
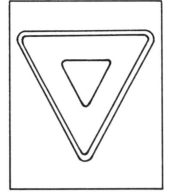

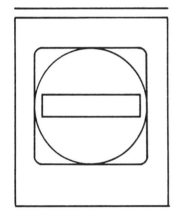

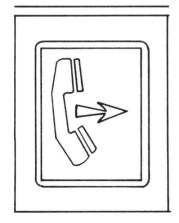

10. Street

Name_____

Date_____

Teacher_____

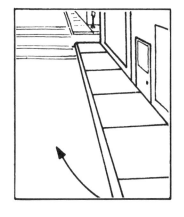
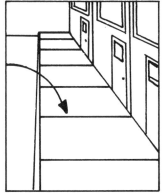

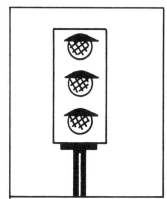

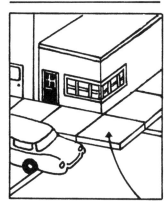
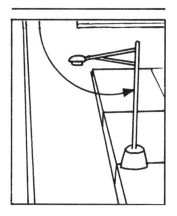

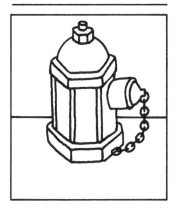

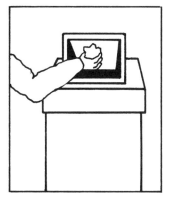
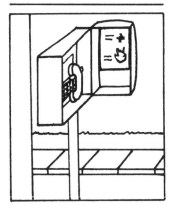

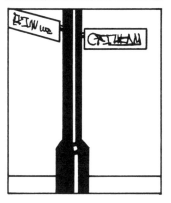

11. Occupations

Name_____

Date_____

Teacher_____

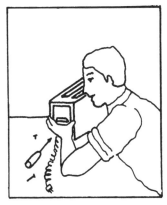

12. Shopping

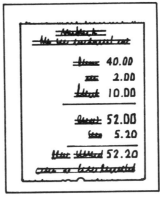

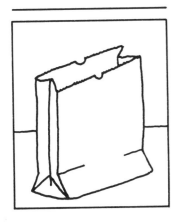

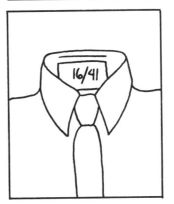
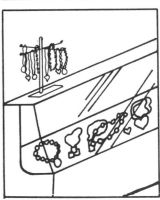

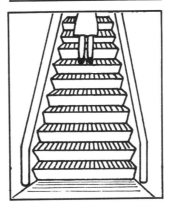
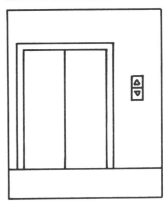

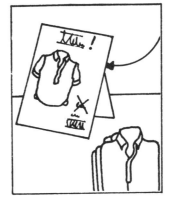

13. Office

Name_____
Date_____
Teacher_____

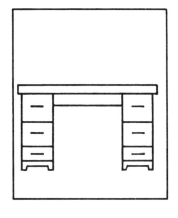

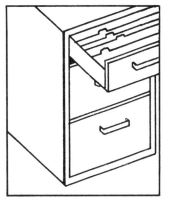

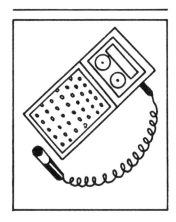

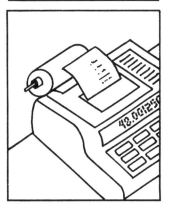
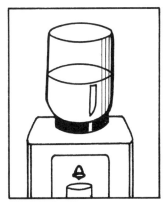

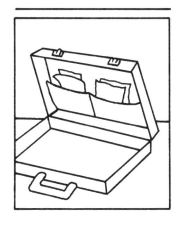
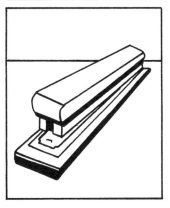
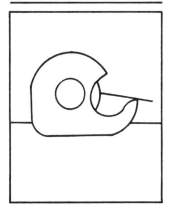
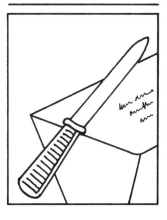

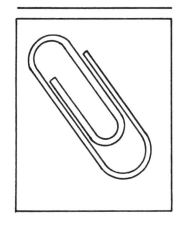
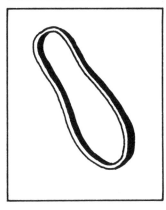
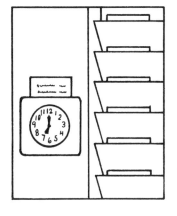
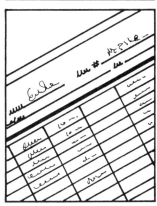

14. Restaurant

Name_____

Date_____

Teacher_____

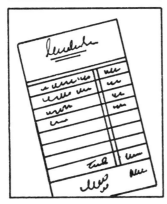

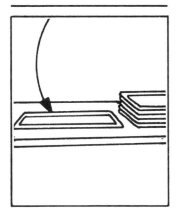
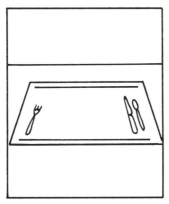

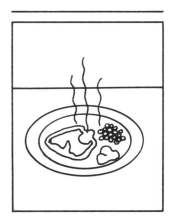

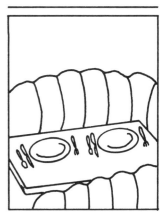

15. Food

Name_____

Date_____

Teacher_____

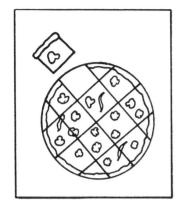
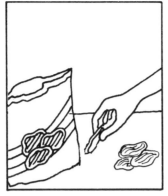
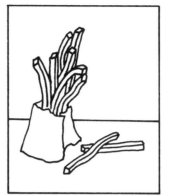

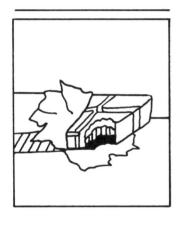
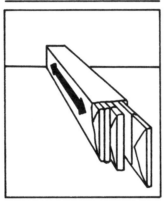
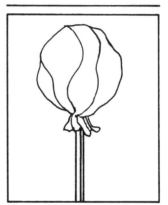

16. Parts of the Body

Name_____

Date_____

Teacher_____

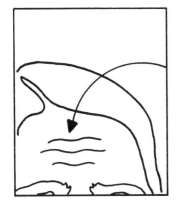 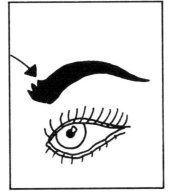 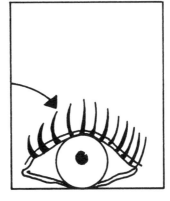 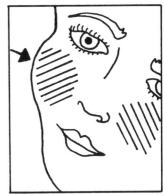

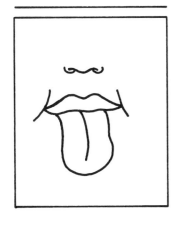  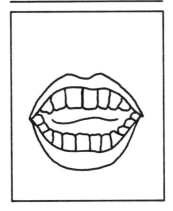 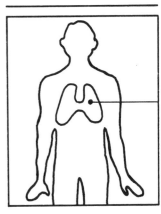

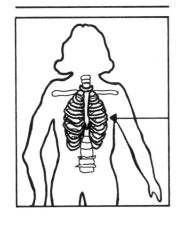 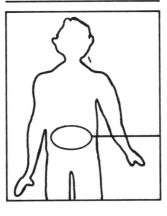 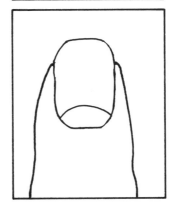 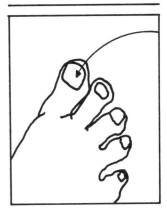

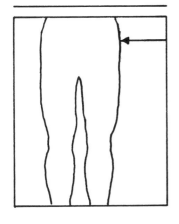 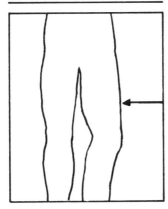 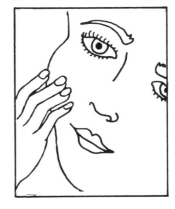 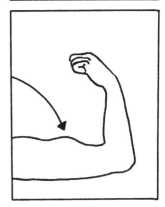

17. Laundromat and Parts of Clothing

Name_____

Date_____

Teacher_____

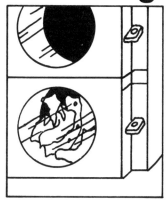
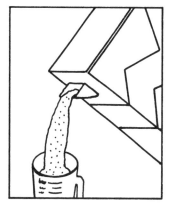
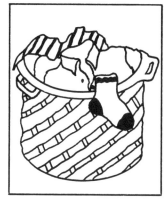

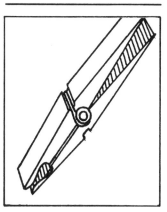

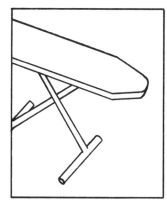

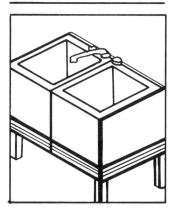
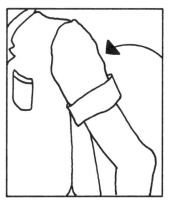
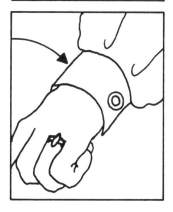
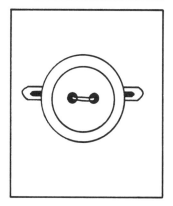

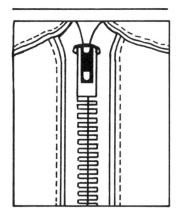
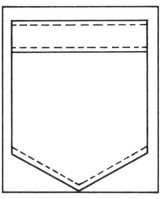
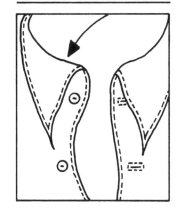
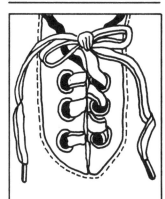

18. Dwelling

Name_____

Date_____

Teacher_____

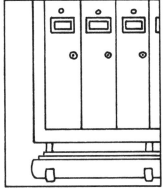
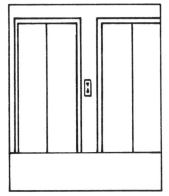
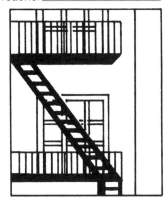

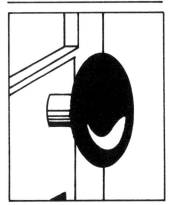
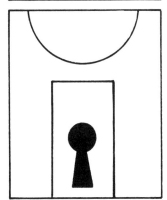
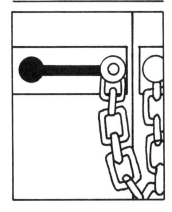

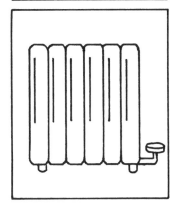
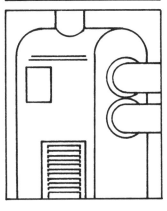
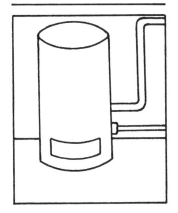
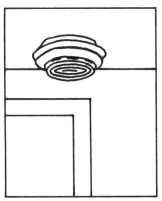

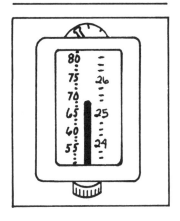
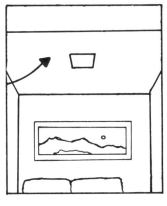
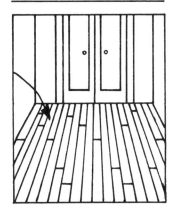

19. Kitchen

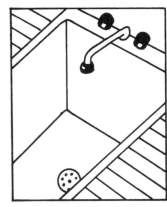

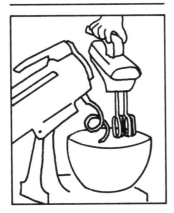

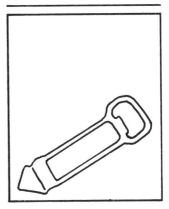

20. Bathroom

Name_____
Date_____
Teacher_____

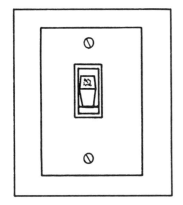

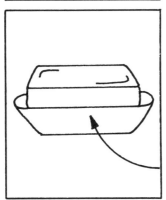
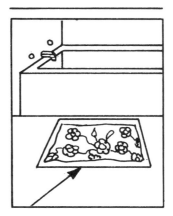
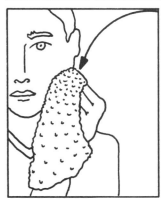

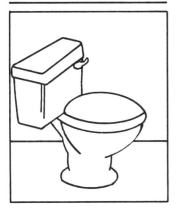
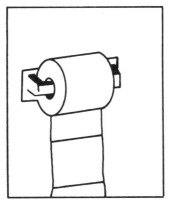
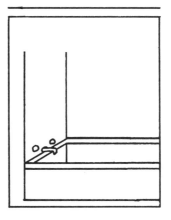

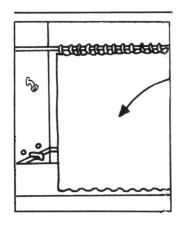
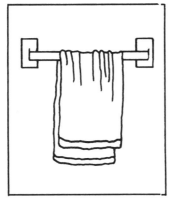
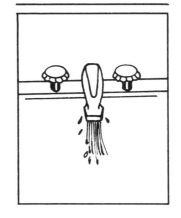
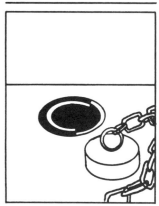

21. Houshold Items

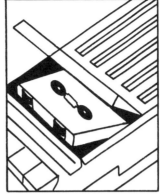
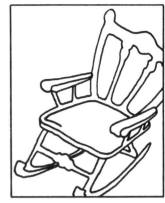
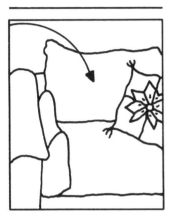
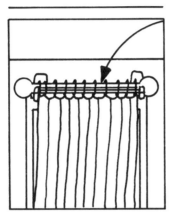
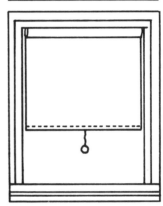
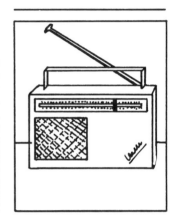

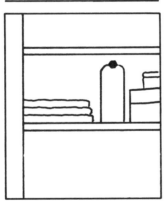
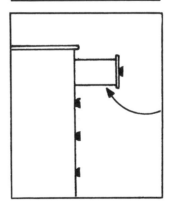
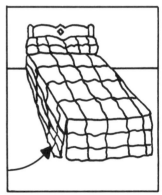
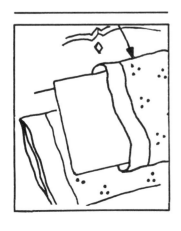
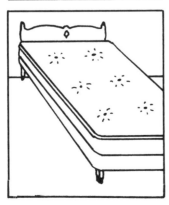
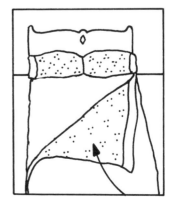
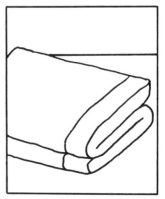

22. Personal Items

Name_____
Date_____
Teacher_____

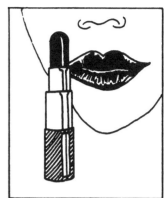

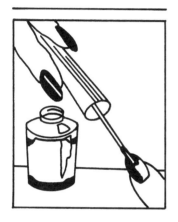
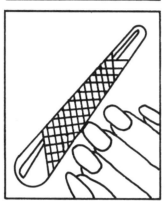
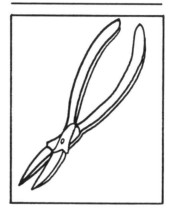
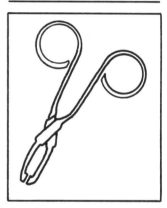

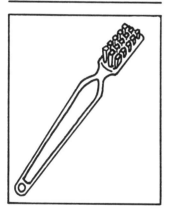
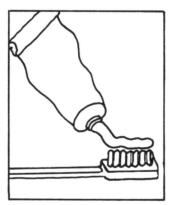
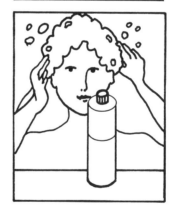
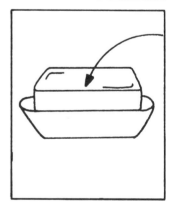

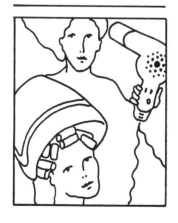
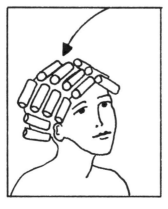

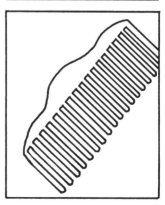

23. Telephone and Television

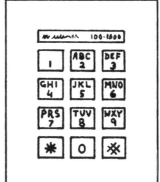

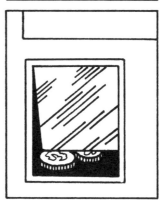

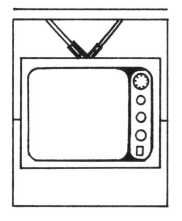
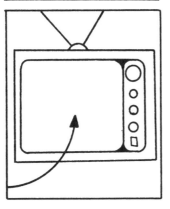
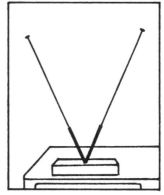
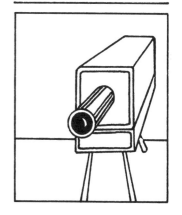

24. Workshop

Name_____
Date_____
Teacher_____

   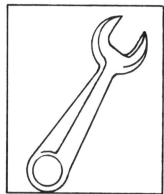

  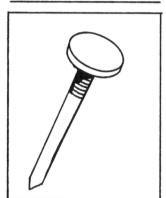 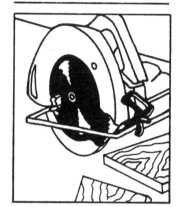

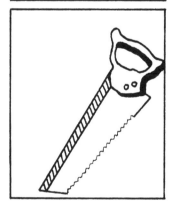 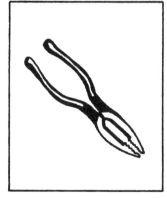 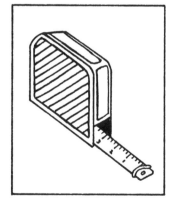 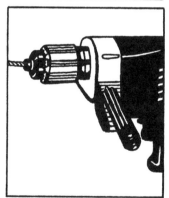

 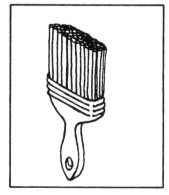  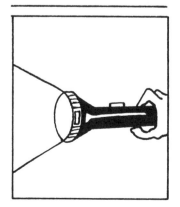

25. Gardening

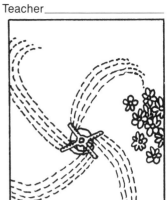

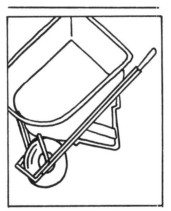

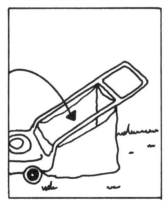
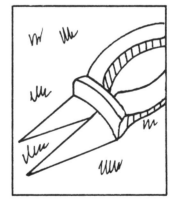
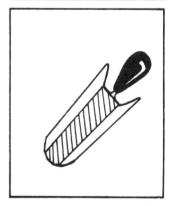

26. Sports Equipment

 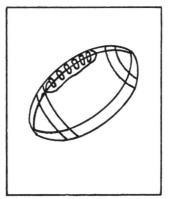 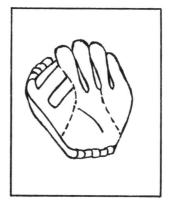 

 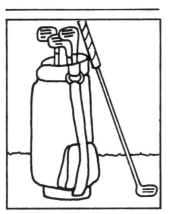  

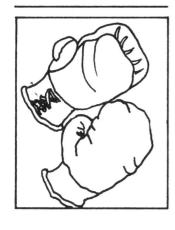 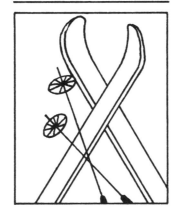 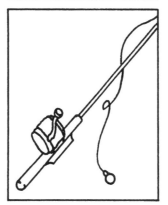 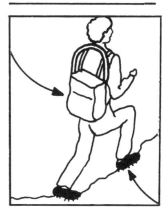

27. Infants

Name_____

Date_____

Teacher_____

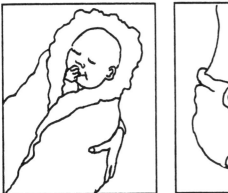 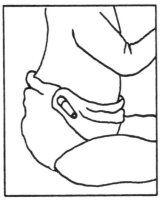 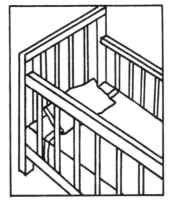 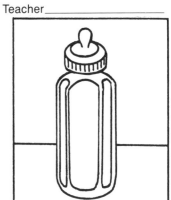

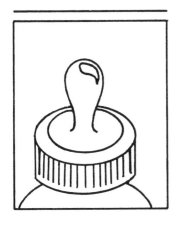  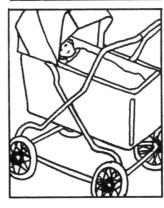 

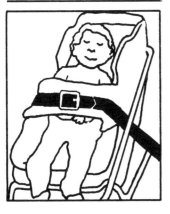   

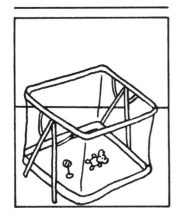 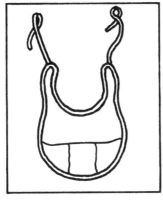  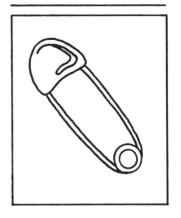

28. Leisure Activities

Name_____

Date_____

Teacher_____

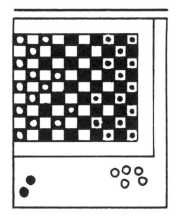

29. Feelings

30. Antonyms

Name_____

Date_____

Teacher_____

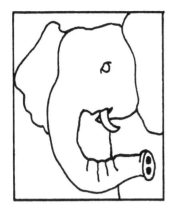   

 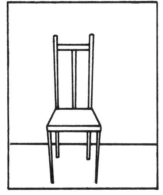  

  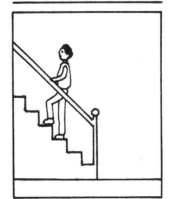

31. Emergencies

Name_____
Date_____
Teacher_____

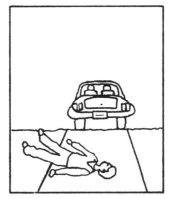

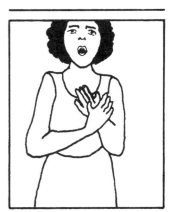

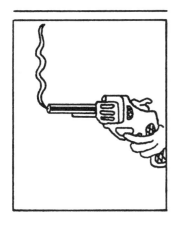
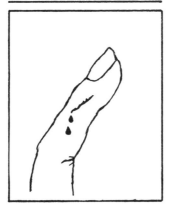

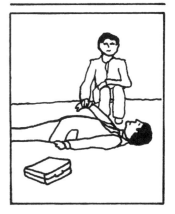

32. Sewing and Hand Crafts

Name_____
Date_____
Teacher_____

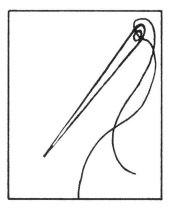 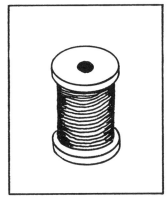 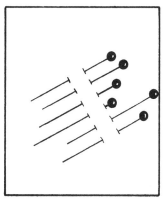 

 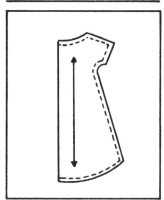  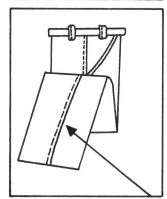

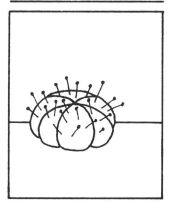  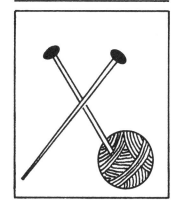 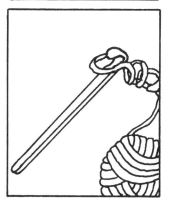

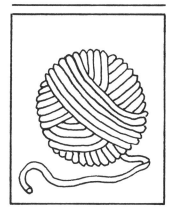 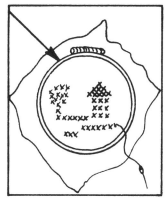 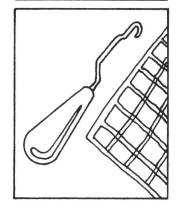 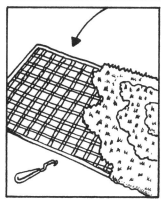